S0-AEG-355

Persist and Publish

Persist and Publish

Helpful Hints for Academic Writing and Publishing

Ralph E. Matkin *and* T. F. Riggar

University Press of Colorado

Copyright © 1991 by the University Press of Colorado
P.O. Box 849
Niwot, Colorado 80544

All rights reserved.

The University Press of Colorado is a cooperative publishing enterprise supported, in part, by Adams State College, Colorado State University, Fort Lewis College, Mesa State College, Metropolitan State College of Denver, University of Colorado, University of Northern Colorado, University of Southern Colorado, and Western State College.

Library of Congress Cataloging-in-Publication Data

Matkin, Ralph E., 1946–
    Persist and publish: helpful hints for academic writing and publishing / Ralph E. Matkin and T. F. Riggar.
        p.   cm.
    Includes bibliographical references and index.
    ISBN 0-87081-227-0 (pbk.)
    1. Scholarly publishing.   2. Learning and scholarship — Authorship.   3. College teachers as authors.   I. Riggar, T. F.   II. Title.
    Z286.S37M38   1991
    070.5 — dc20   91-19028
                                                                                                 CIP

The paper used in this publication meets the minimum requirements of the American National Standard for Information Sciences—Permanence of Paper for Printed Library Materials. ANSI Z39.48–1984
∞

10   9   8   7   6   5   4   3   2   1

To Susan, the one who gives meaning to the words

Contents

Preface

Persist and Publish contains many of the authors' publication experiences and reflections blended with valuable information from other authorities to offer sound methods to increase productivity and achievement in the publish-or-perish academic world. Although the principal focus of the book is for novice academics who wish to begin submitting their writing to local newsletters and journals, considerable information is provided for more experienced professors who desire to publish books and more comprehensive reference materials. Thus, *Persist and Publish* is designed to facilitate and enhance writing activities of new and tenured faculty throughout the entire competitive arena of publishing.

Seldom does a day pass when people in every walk of life do not write something, whether it is simply a reminder note or a lengthy technical report. For those working in academic environments as faculty or students, writing often is an essential part of their respective activities. Few academicians today will deny the importance of developing writing skills and a publication record. These are necessary at most institutions of higher education in order for tenure, promotion, and salary increases to be granted. Although the phrase "publish or perish" is not new, it is becoming more meaningful in a pragmatic sense for academicians whose careers may be advanced or terminated on the basis of publications alone.

The purpose of this book is to provide concise, comprehensive, and practical information focusing on demonstrated methods that enhance manuscript publication. To achieve this, this book discusses underlying reasons for publishing in academic settings (Chapters 1 and 2), identifies basic tools and settings needed to facilitate writing activities (Chapters 3 and 4), and provides easy-to-follow tips for publishing in newsletters (Chapter 5), journals (Chapter 6), monographs and technical reports (Chapter 7), and books (Chapter 8). The remaining chapters are devoted to selected activities that frequently accrue for published authors. Chapter 9, for example, covers creative writing outlets, while Chapter 10 discusses many benefits authors reap from their writing efforts. The book concludes with a bibliography of references cited in the text. The references represent what we believe are the best articles, books, or research studies on the subject. Many of these references provide information that we have experienced both personally and professionally as authors. Furthermore, the bibliography is annotated to provide assistance for readers seeking additional information.

Persist and Publish: Helpful Hints for Academic Writing and Publishing offers readers many "tricks of the trade" when dealing with editors and the publishing process. Figures and tables are used frequently to assist in conceptualizing critical steps of the process. It is assumed that readers understand that good writing style and proper grammar usage are essential ingredients of scholarly writing. Accordingly, *Persist and Publish* is designed to build upon writers' developed communication skills by offering tips that facilitate and enhance the acquisition of personal publication records.

We wish to recognize and express our appreciation to many people who assisted in this endeavor. Foremost are the many students at the Rehabilitation Institute of Southern Illinois University at Carbondale who participated in the graduate course titled "Academic Publishing." Their suggestions and questions helped construct the framework of this book. Support and encouragement were offered by the following colleagues at Southern Illinois University: Dr. Donald Beggs, dean of the College of Education; Dr. William Crimando, past editor and past managing editor of the *Vocational Evaluation and Work Adjustment Bulletin;* Dr. Marilyn Hafer, editorial board member of numerous journals in the rehabilitation field; Dr. Gary Austin, coeditor of the Mary Switzer Memorial Seminar monographs; Dr. Stanford Rubin, nationally known author and recipient of numerous research awards in the rehabilitation field; Linda Patrick, word processing unit of the College of Education; Karen Schmitt, research photography; and graduate assistants Tom Gabert, Steve Arcona, Jill Garrison, Jeff Cartnal, and Lisa Gorski.

Additional support and assistance were provided liberally by the following faculty and staff of California State University, Long Beach: Dr. John Sikula, dean of the Graduate School of Education; Dr. Charles Kokaska, Educational Psychology and Administration; Dr. Robert Boice, director of the Center for Faculty Development; and Dr. Jim

Turner, associate director of the Center for Faculty Development. A special thank you is extended as well to Dr. Geraldine Hansen, Assumption College, and to Dr. Robert Liberman, chief of Rehabilitation Medicine Service of the West Los Angeles Department of Veterans Affairs Medical Center, Brentwood Division.

Finally, a debt of gratitude is owed to Susan Riggar for her copy editing, helpful suggestions, and assistive rewrites. Without her efforts, the process would have not progressed as smoothly, concluded as well, or facilitated the beginning of our future projects.

RALPH E. MATKIN
California State University, Long Beach

T. F. RIGGAR
Southern Illinois University, Carbondale

About the Authors

Dr. Ralph E. Matkin is an associate professor with the Department of Educational Psychology and Administration, Graduate School of Education, California State University, Long Beach. He also holds affiliations as an adjunct research psychologist with the School of Medicine, University of California, Los Angeles, and as data manager for the Rehabilitation Medicine Service of the West Los Angeles Department of Veterans Affairs Medical Center, Brentwood Division. Dr. Matkin has published over sixty articles in peer-reviewed professional journals, as well as numerous consultation reports, book reviews, newsletter articles, and two previous books. Dr. Matkin is a consulting reviewer for five professional journals, among which he serves on three editorial advisory boards.

Dr. T. F. Riggar is a professor at the Rehabilitation Institute, College of Education, Southern Illinois University at Carbondale. Dr. Riggar has published over fifty articles in peer-reviewed professional journals. In addition he has over seventy other publications, such as monographs, newsletter articles, book reviews, and commentaries. Dr. Riggar currently serves on the editorial advisory boards of five professional journals and is a consulting reviewer for two others. This is his tenth book.

In addition to their writing activities, both authors are active participants in their respective campus communities helping colleagues successfully negotiate the scholarly research-teaching-service maze. Dr. Matkin provides mentoring support to new faculty members through the CSULB Office of Faculty Development, and offers educational and computer training to personnel at the West Los Angeles Department of Veterans Affairs Medical Center through the Office of the Chief of Staff. Dr. Riggar teaches a course in academic publishing at SIU-C, chairs the institute's Faculty Productivity Committee, and serves as a member of the Promotion and Tenure Committee.

List of Figures and Tables

Figures

Tables

Persist and Publish

I Wanted to Be a Teacher, Not a Writer

Many new or inexperienced academicians find writing an exciting venture that is or will become an integral part of their careers. For others, it is a job requirement, nothing more. For a few, writing for publication is drudgery, punishment, torture, a stimulus for fear, frustration, rejection, inadequacy, anger, resentment, and depression. This book is designed to aid those who are beginning their professional writing activities as well as those who wish to overcome common problems in attempting to put pen to paper.

Simply put, writing for publication requires practice. What many academicians fail to realize, however, is that practice does not have to be painful. In fact, the secret to writing practice is to be aware that it constantly occurs whenever one writes a note to another, jots a self-reminder, composes a letter, creates reports at work, and proofreads final drafts, to mention a few daily activities. Any writing activity is a method of practicing the art of communication because writers want their messages to be understood by their intended recipients. Writing for professional academic publication has the same intention, although the intended audience is generally larger, and attention must be given to the formatting requirements indicated by publishers.

The general public regards academicians as experienced and knowledgeable about their fields. Indeed, becoming an expert in a chosen discipline is an ongoing process that may take a long time to acquire. Likewise, the ability to communicate knowledge, novel ideas, theories, and practical applications effectively is a learned skill that requires practice. Although the writings of others are the bases of an expert's knowledge and can serve as models of necessary writing skills, seldom is technical writing proficiency acquired through reading alone. Boice and Johnson (1984) stressed this point, noting that professional academic writing is as separate an arena of expertise as any other field, although rarely is it taught as part of, or in conjunction with, most advanced degrees.

We are constantly amazed when we discover competent academicians who do not know the reasons for or methods of disseminating their expertise. Years spent learning, studying, and assimilating knowledge appear in no way to prepare them to communicate it effectively to others. When we looked back on our own careers, for example, it became clear that our respective doctoral programs failed to prepare us for subsequent employment in academia. While both programs prepared us well to become practitioners, only one required teaching. Further, doctoral students in that program were required to teach for two years while students in the other one were seldom offered such opportunities. One program emphasized research and publications by its students, with most graduates departing with one or two publications (usually in collaboration with their major advisor), while the other emphasized courses in measurement and statistics but provided neither guidance nor encouragement for publication. Neither program seriously considered preparation for or exposure to professional service outlets.

Improving graduate student writing through seminars, workshops, classes, and mentoring is rare in academia (Figgins and Burbach 1989; Greaser 1979; O'Brien and Johnson 1980; Reitt 1980). In the absence of this, aspiring authors frequently turn to a variety of sources to learn how to write and publish (many of which are contained in the Annotated Bibliography).

The purpose of this chapter is to define "academic writing" and compare its characteristics to another form of communication associated with knowledge dissemination — teaching. Among the points covered in the chapter are: (1) types of scholarly publications, (2) components of manuscripts directed to different types of publications, and (3) similarities and differences of manuscript components and other methods of communication. The goal of the chapter is to help

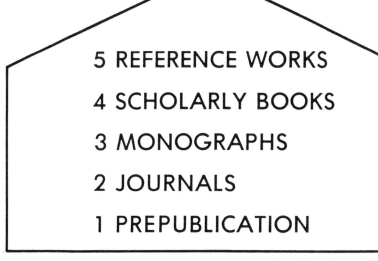

5 REFERENCE WORKS

4 SCHOLARLY BOOKS

3 MONOGRAPHS

2 JOURNALS

1 PREPUBLICATION

Figure 1.1. Types of scholarly publishing. Adapted from R. W. Funk. 1977. Issues in scholarly publishing. *Scholarly Publishing* 9(1): 3–17. Reprinted with permission of University of Toronto Press.

readers understand that many of their acquired skills and abilities are transferrable to writing activities.

Types of Scholarly Publications

For the purposes of this book, academic writing is defined as the discovery, production, publication, and dissemination of scholarly knowledge. Discovery refers to accepted methods specified by occupational disciplines through which professionals encounter, explore, and/or create phenomena. Academic disciplines adhere to variations of the scientific method of inquiry which involves systematic examination of information or products in order to learn new information. Production relies on the properties of shape and form to give evidence of discovered ideas, concepts, theories, and applications. Publication is a method of disseminating scholarly and popular information about discoveries and outcomes.

Publishing exists in many forms and on various levels. Figure 1.1 shows the most common hierarchy in academic writing. Level 1, for

5

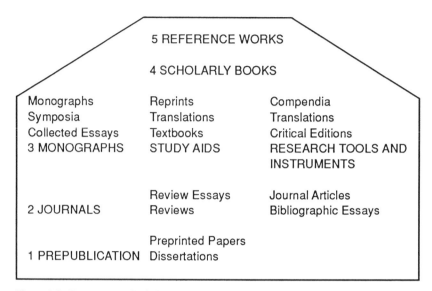

Figure 1.2. Components of scholarly publishing. Adapted from R. W. Funk. 1977. Issues in scholarly publishing. *Scholarly Publishing* 9(1): 3–17. Reprinted with permission of University of Toronto Press.

example, involves the discovery-production stage of scholarly knowledge, followed by the first formal academic publication outlet, journal articles. As one progresses up the list, works generally increase in length and substance. This model, however, is based neither on quality and quantity nor time and effort required for manuscript completion. Instead, it is founded on a developmental process that involves acquiring knowledge and learning. As one proceeds from book reports and papers written in elementary and high school to undergraduate term papers to graduate research reports, a subtle learning process shapes the style of and motivation for writing. In the same way, the progression to academic publishing follows a developmental path building on earlier writing experiences. Seldom does successful publishing achievement come without prior assistance, although sometimes it is difficult to recall the many individuals and advice given that provided guidance and structure.

Figure 1.2 expands the academic writing hierarchy by revealing many examples of works that make up the first three levels. Although writers may start at any level, beginning authors soon discover that practice, patience, and starting with short manuscripts will, with persistence, eventually lead to longer more complex works. The model in both figures is deceptively simple, particularly among those who, after completing a master's thesis or doctoral dissertation, may believe that a book of a few hundred pages is a "natural" next step in writing. A fifteen- to twenty-page manuscript submitted for publication as an article (generally yielding no more than four or five printed pages) requires a good deal of preliminary writing.

Often beginning authors only see the end product of the academic writing process. Other portions of the process may be observed when, as students, they work as teaching assistants or when they participate in studies conducted by professors. More often than not, though, many of the "invisible" steps crucial to the product are not apparent. For example, who sees the hours devoted to conceptualizing an idea, researching references, writing notes, outlining topics, writing first drafts, rewriting and editing, submitting the manuscript, waiting for acceptance (or rejection), rewriting for clarification and final editorial approval, and reading and correcting galley proofs prior to publication? This is not at all glamorous stuff, but it is, nevertheless, essential for those who write for publication.

Components of Manuscripts

Each scholarly publication has its own format, often derived from recognized writing manuals developed or adopted by professional disciplines or publishers. For example, the Modern Language Association (guides for the humanities), American Psychological Association (guides for applied and behavioral sciences), American Medical Association (guides for medical and physical sciences), and the American Bar Association (guides for the legal profession) provide acceptable (albeit different) standardized writing formats for their respective constituencies. For the purposes of this book, *Chicago Manual of Style* (13th edition) is used because of its general, widespread acceptance among contemporary publishers of academic periodicals and books. Another popular standardized format is that based on the Publication Manual of the American Psychological Association (3d edition). This

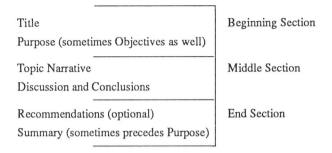

Title	Beginning Section
Purpose (sometimes Objectives as well)	
Topic Narrative	Middle Section
Discussion and Conclusions	
Recommendations (optional)	End Section
Summary (sometimes precedes Purpose)	

Figure 1.3. Elements of prepublications.

APA format is also used in many journals as their preferred style of publishing articles. Indeed, would-be authors should become familiar with appropriate writing manuals required by the editors of targeted publications.

Prepublications

There are many form and style requirements for an acceptable term paper, master's thesis, or doctoral dissertation — the prepublications referred to in Figures 1.1 and 1.2. (Additional examples of prepublications include book reports, periodic work reports, consultation reports, letters to the editor, "in-brief" articles, and newsletter columns.) For the many types of manuscripts contained in this category, there are an equivalent number of components within them. Why? One reason is that different audiences may have different needs that affect written presentation of materials (e.g., an executive summary preface, a "bottom line" presentation, a technical anthology supporting derived conclusions). Most importantly, however, prepublications are individualized, seldom standardized stylistically beyond the relatively small audience for which they are intended, seldom reviewed impartially and blindly prior to publication, seldom made available for scrutiny by the general public, frequently of varied length and technical complexity, and, for the purposes of this book, seldom weighted heavily on one's publication record in academia.

Prepublications, nevertheless, are important for several reasons: (1) Their substance may have critical relevance for facilitating effective group communication. (2) The methods used to disseminate information reflect presenters' abilities to communicate effectively.

(3) Recipients of prepublications may request reprints for subsequent publication. (4) They represent methods by which authors practice and polish their writing skills. Accordingly, prepublications generally incorporate the elements listed in Figure 1.3.

All publications share a common framework composed of a beginning, a middle, and an end. Depending on editorial styles, however, the summary elements, typically at the end of manuscripts, sometimes begin a document. Examples of prefacing summaries are abstracts, executive summaries, and overviews. Thus, a wise author first checks the desired or required formatting style for specific prepublications. If a small amount of time is devoted to learning the preferred format, there may be less frustration encountered because the manuscript may not have to be rewritten.

Journals

Writing for publication in the academic world most frequently means having one's manuscripts appear in journals of professional associations. Figure 1.2 reveals that in addition to journal articles, this category includes review essays, book reviews, and bibliographic essays. Journal articles, however, represent the bulk of the content. With over 70,000 professional journals published throughout the world (Day 1988), the opportunities for publishing are nearly boundless. The average published article does not usually exceed four to six printed pages in most journals. Four to six pages of printed material usually translates to between fifteen and twenty double-spaced typewritten manuscript pages. In some fields and in some journals these numbers and sizes are doubled. A twenty- to forty-page manuscript results in an average article of some eight to twelve pages. Table 1.1 reveals the typical elements of most academic journal articles.

As noted in Table 1.1, the basic structure of a journal article depends on the nature of the material: Does it present research data or theoretical information? These frameworks generally are not applicable for reviews and essays, both of which tend to require a general narrative composed of the following elements: Title, Purpose, Topical Discussion, Conclusion, and Recommendations (optional). Furthermore, reviews generally do not exceed four to six double-spaced typewritten pages.

Structure	Content

Theoretical and Practice Articles

Structure	Content
Title Page	Concise description of theme
Biographical Sketch (optional)	Author's credentials and affiliations
Abstract	Short summary of content, generally seventy-five words or less
Introduction	Brief literature review and purpose
Topical Narrative	Expansion on topics germane to the stated purpose
Discussion	Relates topics to previous literature
Summary and Recommendations	Conclusions and proposed directions
References	Acknowledgment of only those cited
Tables and Figures	Outlines and drawings used in text

Research and Empirical Investigations

Structure	Content
Title Page	Same as above
Biographical Sketch (optional)	Same as above
Introduction	Same as above
Methodology	Instruments used, participants, data collection procedures used, analyses
Results	Reported outcomes achieved
Discussion	Interpretation of results in relation to previous literature, limitations
Conclusions	Proposed directions
References	Same as above
Tables and Figures	Same as above

Table 1.1. Elements of academic journal articles.

Monographs

Many authors write a monograph as a first work. It is more common, however, for such works to be produced over considerable time and with continued study. In typewritten form, these manuscripts generally contain at least 40 pages and possibly as many as 150, although the typical length usually does not exceed 60 to 80 pages. It

Title Page

Foreword

Preface

Table of Contents

List of Tables and Figures

Steering Committee, Project Staff, Consultants, Review Teams, etc.

Abstract

Overview of the Project

Literature Review

Project Activities

Results and Discussion

Conclusions and Recommendations

Dissemination and Utilization Plan

References

Appendices

Figure 1.4. Elements of monographs.

is not uncommon for manuscripts that are intended for monograph publication to be single-spaced instead of double-spaced. Figure 1.2 provides several examples of materials considered to be monographs.

It is not uncommon for monographs to be printed "in-house." That is to say, monographs written by one or more collaborative authors usually do not receive extensive review beyond the editor or staff of the publishing firm or university department prior to printing. Frequently the information contained in monographs is extremely technical or of

Title Page

Table of Contents

List of Tables and Figures

Foreword

Preface

Chapters

    Title

    Major Headings

    Minor Headings

    Subheadings

    Tables and Figures (as appropriate)

Glossary (optional)

Appendices (as appropriate)

References

Index

Figure 1.5. Elements of scholarly books.

such focused interest that dissemination is limited to a relatively small number of people. More often than not, the cost of printing and dissemination is subsidized through public funds awarded through local, state, or national grants. Because of the diverse formatting requirements associated with such publications, Figure 1.4 provides only a general approximation of the elements found in monographs.

Scholarly Books

For most new authors, the idea of writing a book comes to mind immediately following the publication of a journal article. Scholarly books (including textbooks) frequently represent a distillation of years of work, research activity, experience, and writing practice. Such books are composed of various individual topics discussed at length and built around a common theme that is usually identified in a book's preface and often found in chapter overviews and summaries.

Unlike experienced writers, new authors often believe initially that writing a book is 90 percent inspiration and 10 percent perspiration, the latter represented by quantity and not quality. Put another way, many a first-time writer often believes a book is an opportunity to include material that was deleted from a journal article manuscript in preparation for its publication. Others (including at one time one of this book's authors) naively believe that their master's thesis or doctoral dissertation is sufficient material from which a book will emerge. In retrospect, however, the above author found that his dissertation constituted significantly less than one chapter in his first book. Perhaps the best way for a new author to plan writing a first magnum opus is to begin by rereading a familiar book and thinking of it in terms of its style, readability, manner of presentation, and general appeal. These tips can be helpful first steps in conceptualizing what aspects of a book could be improved upon as the reader embarks on becoming an author.

We have found considerable disagreement regarding the definition of a book. As noted in Figure 1.2, textbooks are listed above journals yet below scholarly books. Our experience authoring, coauthoring, editing, and coediting over a dozen books is that such works range considerably in their scholarly intent and nature. Beth Luey (1987), a very accomplished author and editor, notes that some schools, deans,

---

Title Page

Table of Contents

List of Contributors (as appropriate)

List of Tables and Figures

Preface

Acknowledgments

Major Parts (containing related chapters)

    Chapters

        Overview

        Major Headings

        Subheadings

        Tables and Figures (as appropriate)

        Summary

        Implications/Changes (from previous editions, as appropriate)

Appendices (as appropriate)

References

Index

Figure 1.6. Elements of reference works.

and administrators "mistakenly view textbook writing as non-scholarly activity" (p. 3). Given such an environment, we have found that some advantages and rewards noted in Chapter 2 may be diminished and authors may wish to disregard some publishing avenues.

Reference Works

At the pinnacle of Figures 1.1 and 1.2 is the reference work. These are books that summarize a field or academic area in a format that is comprehensive and easy to follow. One such book in the field of rehabilitation, for example, is George N. Wright's *Total Rehabilitation*. Another, representing the field of psychology, is Buro's *Mental Measurement Yearbook*. These references literally cover every major area defined by their respective specializations, thus allowing readers to gain sufficient information to seek more detailed materials covering specific aspects as needed. Reference works involve the most time and effort to compile. It is not unusual for more than five years to pass between subsequent editions. Although Figures 1.5 and 1.6 appear very similar, the difference between scholarly books and reference works is substantive. Because of the time involved to compile, write, edit, and print books, the materials contained in them may be at least two or three years old in relation to the copyright date.

In the overall textbook-scholarly book-reference work hierarchy we have found that the specific field and its respected senior members, all of whom publish significantly, make final scholarly quality determinations. Levitt and Naas (1989) note that the field itself "puts the lid on" the garbage can processes in publishing (p. 191). Our experience makes it clear that aside from the occasional envious remark, senior professionals who have done similar work can make needed objective assessments. Basically the "evaluation of scholarly authors relies heavily on the reputation and judgment of scholarly publishers" (Luey 1989, p. 80). We have learned to take great care as to who "has been around a long time" and who is a "senior with credible publishing experience." As noted in our last chapter, many pretend but few attain.

Writing and Teaching: Similarities and Differences

Writers and teachers strive to achieve a common goal — knowledge transfer through effective use of communication methods. Fortunately "the attributes of excellence in teaching and writing are remarkably similar" (Jalongo 1987, p. 49). As will be noted, many of the traits and dimensions that lead to success in one endeavor also lead to accomplishment in the other. Publications represent written communications used to instruct others, whereas teaching uses both written and oral presentation methods. In order to be effective, a teacher must use both forms to convey information to students with individual learning patterns. For example, some people learn best when left alone to read while others seem to learn best when participating in "hands-on" activities. Effective teachers plan for such diverse learning styles when preparing lesson plans and class assignments.

Course syllabi, lesson plans, and class assignments are examples of written activities teachers use to communicate information to students. Like manuscripts prepared for publication, written class materials are used to set the stage for students, communicate a sense of subject coverage expected by a course of instruction, identify goals of the class and performance expectations, and provide an outline by which the course can be evaluated. When tests and quizzes are incorporated into course work, their content must be communicated clearly and concisely (just as in manuscript writing) in order to facilitate achievement of correct responses.

Unlike manuscript preparation, however, teaching includes auditory as well as visual presentation. Each of us remembers those teachers whose verbal and "performing" styles made learning fun, those who brought life and meaning to subjects that we dreaded or were certain would be dry and boring. Similarly, each of us recalls those subjects that indeed were more effective than the best sleeping potion prescribed for insomnia.

Written manuscripts seldom can capture the vitality of "live" communication. At best, written presentations (whether class syllabi, tests, or articles) can enhance conceptualization depending on the methods selected by authors. Often the most appropriate methods selected depend on the audiences for which written communications are intended, which may include use of figures, graphs, tables, pictures, colloquial expressions, professional jargon, precise terminology, popularly defined words and phrases, and simple or complex sentences. Written materials communicate most effectively when readers understand what authors intend. Effective teaching relies on the same principle.

Publish or Perish Is the Name of the Game

Teaching, service, and writing are activities that go hand in hand for most academic positions. Seldom, however, are the three weighted equally in desirability among academicians or in determining rewards in an academic setting (Boice 1987b; Thompson 1987a, 1987b). This chapter discusses the reasons institutions of higher learning seem to favor faculty publication activities when making retention, tenure, and promotion decisions. Why academic writing is required, the key determinants of practice, and the rewards of writing are among the points covered.

Why Academic Writing Is Required

Why do universities around the world require their faculties to publish? Based upon the definition of academic writing in Chapter 1, the answer is as simple as it is clear — to demonstrate production and discovery of scholarly knowledge through public means of dissemination, i.e., publication. It is the business of universities to discover, produce, publish, and disseminate scholarly knowledge by its faculty through printed media. In addition to their graduates (and athletic teams), university reputations are built on the quality and quantity of scholarly contributions to the fields of art and science, as well as through grant applications and awards. School prestige often affects both quantity and quality of student and faculty applicants.

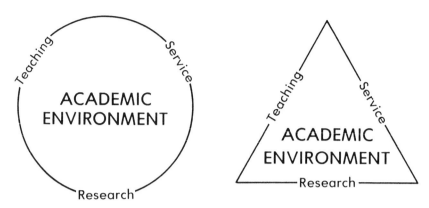

Figure 2.1. Two models of the teaching-research-service paradigm.

Universities are not the only producers of knowledge, research, and publications. Notable centers such as Bell Laboratories, Argonne National Laboratory, Brookings Institute, the Urban Institute, the Dupont Corporation, various governmental agencies, and many other public and private businesses and industries discover, produce, and disseminate knowledge. Universities, however, consistently and constantly consolidate research and publication with their roles in teaching and service activities. University research and writing not only are designed to produce new and "better" knowledge, but also to cultivate minds that generate more effective and efficient knowledge in the future.

Figure 2.1 presents two models of the teaching-research-service paradigm that we discovered are currently in place at universities. The circular configuration represents a symbiotic interrelationship in which each component leads to and enhances the others. Each part appears to be equally important. The triangular design represents a closer approximation to reality, whereby research forms the foundation for both teaching and service. Since the areas of teaching and service each consist of several parts, their respective relationships with research deserve brief explanation.

Teaching

At most universities, teaching is divided into four parts: didactic courses (teaching-lecture classes), experiential courses (practica-internship-fieldwork classes), independent study courses (working with individuals or small groups on specialized topics), and teaching support (student advisement, theses advisement, and the like). Each area requires knowledge and information acquired from academic publications, such as occupational (professional) journals, monographs, and books. Information from these sources, combined with experience, is transmitted to students in teaching environments.

According to Hosford (1990) and Weaver (1982), undertaking scholarly writing projects promotes better topical comprehension of one's occupational field. Faculty members who conduct research activities are more apt to stay current with their professional literature than faculty who rely solely on their own personal or professional experiences. On the other hand, Friedrich and Michalak (1983) discovered only a slight positive correlation between faculty research and writing accomplishments, and student evaluations of teaching effectiveness. Given the many variables subsumed by "teaching effectiveness," such as manner of presentation, tone of voice, and teacher-student interaction, it is safe to say that keeping current with one's area of expertise at least enhances effective teaching.

In our opinion there exists some truth to the expectation of the "quality researcher-poor teacher" myth. Both as students and as professors we have observed that well-known people who appear constantly in print often present poorly in the classroom. Conversely, some excellent teaching is conducted by academics who never have and probably never will attempt to publish. Part of this problem arises from personal interest, time pressures, and the reward system. Sometimes the problem occurs because people tend to gravitate toward what they enjoy doing the most. We have both enjoyed listening to a well-rehearsed and well-conducted oratory by someone who obviously never read the pertinent literature. Students in the front row appreciate the smooth delivery, funny stories, cute jokes, and fancy overheads, while the senior faculty in the last row know the data are dated and obsolete.

Service

A similar relationship exists between academic writing and faculty service activities. Academic service consists of three parts: service to one's university, one's profession, and the public. University service is divided further to include activities supporting one's unit, the college

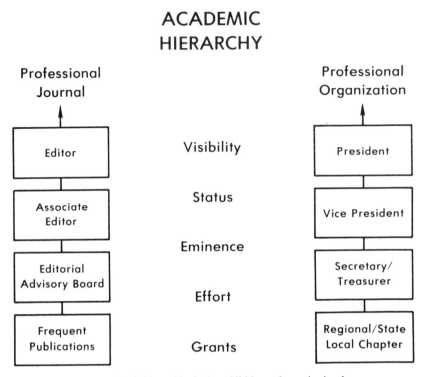

Figure 2.2. Academic hierarchies in the publishing and organizational arenas.

or school, and the total institution. According to Showalter (1978), university service and its functional activities primarily are what distinguish comprehensive universities from liberal arts colleges. Universities that operate in a "publish-or-perish" manner generally tend to obtain and retain those whom Showalter calls "avowed cosmopolitans." Colleges tend to reinforce commitment to and participation in the school rather than an academic field. Although all higher education must reach multiple audiences (e.g., recruit students and raise funds)(Sachs 1988), the publish-or-perish model encourages and stimulates interacademic rather than intra-academic competition designed to minimize, prevent, and eliminate knowledge stagnation (Showalter 1978).

Service to one's profession is demonstrated in the two models of academic hierarchy shown in Figure 2.2. Approximately equal time commitment, involvement, and effort are required at each parallel level for professional service to either an organization or a journal. Finally, public service can include consultation to businesses, organizations, and individuals at community, state, regional, or national levels whether offered gratis or for a fee. The relationship between research/writing and service is that generally the latter is requested by others more frequently the more one becomes known to colleagues and the public through published works. Clearly "getting published . . . helps establish credibility in a chosen profession" (Riggar and Matkin 1990, p. 17).

We constructed Figure 2.2 based on parallel levels of time commitment, involvement, and effort. One aspect we feel worth mentioning is that service to a professional organization is generally the result of an elective process, i.e., you must be elected to office. Appointment to a professional journal, however, very rarely results from elections; it depends mostly on "blind," peer-refereed competence in research and writing.

Key Determinants

Time and Place Ingredients

What elements shape a person to become a writer? What are some of the ingredients in terms of time requirements, length and types of experiences, amount of effort, and timing? Fortunately, there are many studies that examine these questions and provide some insight. One of the first ingredients noted is that those who start writing early in their careers seem to produce the most and continue writing longest (Clemente 1973; Cole and Cole 1967; Hickson, Stacks, and Armsbary 1989; Rodgers and Maranto 1989). However, the age of writers in relation to their academic rank appears to be an inconclusive variable. For example, Riggs (1978) found that often assistant professors have the highest rate of writing and publishing, while other studies indicate that full professors are most productive (Aleamoni and Yimer 1973; Bayer and Dutton 1977; Walton 1982). These outcomes confirm that junior faculty, such as assistant professors, may indeed write the most at any given time (rate) in their quest for promotion and tenure. Yet, these same faculty members are perhaps the youngest among their colleagues, accounting for less overall numbers of published manuscripts (productivity) than their senior (and presumably older) faculty professors (Jones, Preusz, and Finkelstein 1989).

Discussion of time involves more than chronological age or the number of years one's career spans. Research findings suggest that the single largest impediment to academic writing and research is the amount of time allocated for such activities by academicians and/or their employers (i.e., universities).

Although many high-volume writers indicate a preference to teach rather than do research and write (Walton 1982), classroom activities are described as a "tremendous drain" on the time needed for writing (Sorcinelli 1985, p. 1). Whether this complaint is simply a statement of fact or a convenient excuse for inadequate time management, investigators indicate "lack of time" as the major obstacle for research and writing among 36 to 71 percent of faculty surveyed (Boice and Johnson 1984; Walton 1982).

Table 2.1 reveals the average number of hours devoted per week to research and (presumably) concomitant writing efforts. From the table, between 42 and 95 percent of faculty members surveyed spend fewer than thirteen hours each week engaged in research activities, among which, between 13 and 81 percent spend less than five hours each week (Bayer and Dutton 1977; Walton 1982). These figures do not indicate the number of hours used as the base rate, whether a forty-hour work week or the 168 hours available in a seven-day week. There are faculty members who work on research and writing projects during nontraditional working hours (e.g., weekends, vacations, leisure, or family time). In all likelihood, their numbers probably are as few as the percentage of persons in Table 2.1 who report spending more than twenty hours per week on such activities. The question that remains unanswered, however, is what interferes with the majority's commitment to research and writing.

After surveying nearly every faculty member at a major university, Boice and Johnson (1984) discovered that about 56 percent have sporadic writing habits, 25 percent follow a regular weekly writing routine, and about 13 percent set time aside daily to write. Furthermore, 82 percent indicated that they vary the time of day for writing, and about 60 percent report they write in different locations such as the

	Bayer and Dutton 1977			Walton 1982		Boice and Johnson 1984
	0–4 yrs. career age	5–10 yrs. career age	11–25 yrs. career age	High Productivity	Low	Entire Faculty*
	(%)	(%)	(%)	(%)	(%)	(%)
4 hrs. or less	20.0	13.3	16.7	45.8	81.4	45.0
5–12 hrs.	35.1	29.0	30.3	44.6	14.0	27.0
13–20 hrs.	27.5	31.7	29.4	9.6	4.6	19.0
21+ hrs.	17.4	26.0	23.6	—	—	9.0

*Note: "Less than a quarter of this sample claimed a recent total of 10 or more publications" (p. 40).

Table 2.1. Hours per week spent on research.

library, at home, and their offices. Fifty-six percent of the participants need a nondistracting quiet place to write, while others found that goal setting, seclusion, and an established schedule facilitate their writing activities (63, 34, and 32 percent, respectively). Moreover, Boice and Johnson (1984) discovered that most participants report their own writing experiences assist in developing writing habits (86 percent), while 51 percent credited reviewers' comments as additional sources of assistance.

Finally, the vast majority of participants report revising their written drafts at least two times prior to publication.

Career Writing Productivity

While the foregoing research provides some hints concerning aspects writers find helpful when preparing manuscripts, other studies reveal productivity patterns expected by academic institutions. According to

Bayer and Dutton (1977), over 53 percent of the faculty they surveyed have published eleven or more articles, with 32 percent credited with twenty-one or more publications. Boice and Johnson (1984) revealed that nearly 42 percent of the faculty they surveyed have published seven or more manuscripts over a three-year period, with 24 percent having ten or more publications during that time span. Centra (1983) conducted studies focusing on publication productivity among faculty from nonresearch-oriented schools where little emphasis is placed on writing. Over a five-year period, less than two publications per faculty member resulted, compared to two and a half publications generated per faculty member in schools where research is given more emphasis, though is not part of the missions of either type of school (Centra 1983). Depending on the level of institutional and departmental research and writing support it is not unlikely or unreasonable for institutions with high expectations to require two or more referred journal articles per year. Schools with low or moderate publication expectations cite one or fewer refereed articles per year with tenure in five to seven years (Goodwin 1988). To reinforce this observation King (1989) operationally defined ten types of articles and examined 2,541 articles in 375 journals. Approximately half (49 percent) of the authors contributed to empirical articles while over 60 percent contributed to nonempirical articles (p. 287).

In 1962, Voeks revealed that approximately 19 percent of university faculty have ever written, coauthored, revised, or edited a book. More recently, Bayer and Dutton (1977) found that approximately 22 percent of university faculty have written at least three books during their careers, with nearly 10 percent having five or more books or monographs to their individual credit. The most current study available through the American Council of Learned Societies (ACLS 1989) discovered that 78 percent of all academics had authored or coauthored at least one journal article. This is compared to 53 percent for scholars in government, business, and so on. The study further found that 47 percent of academics had published at least one scholarly book, and 29 percent had edited a scholarly book.

Silverman (1984) discovered that senior (first) authorship among university students accounted for less than 2 percent of published manuscripts when authorship was shared with faculty members. Perhaps another sobering finding for beginning writers concerns productivity rates of Nobel laureates compared to other academic authors. According to Zuckerman (1967), Nobel laureates publish nearly three times the number of articles each year compared to others in university settings (3.9 and 1.4, respectively). Indeed, "the most prolific laureate has managed to get out 10.4 papers annually — one every five weeks — for more than 20 years" (p. 393).

Although examples of Nobel laureate writing productivity may represent an ideal few authors will attain, Zuckerman's findings reveal helpful hints for novice writers. "Laureates are more apt to collaborate, with 62% of their papers being multi-authored compared with 51% of the papers by . . . the age-matched (nonlaureate) group" (p. 393). Moreover, it appears that these distinguished professors engage in collaborative writing projects with junior colleagues in much the same way they did earlier in their careers. Clearly, junior faculty should seek productive writers who wish to share their experiences, skills, and encouragement for scholarly activities.

It is our experience that faculty productivity (hours per week spent on research) depends primarily on two factors. The first of these is the level of institutional and departmental research and writing support. This tends to be a universitywide, college, and/or departmental emphasis tied to the notion of "publish or perish." This more global mandate is influenced by the second factor — the support of specific deans and other administrators. As seen in Figure 2.2, the academic hierarchy is composed of the professional journal route and the professional organization avenue. The time, effort, and competence required for administration of professional organizations are more akin to university administration than is the professional journal process. Many university administrators gain their early management experience with professional field-specific organizations before moving on to more generic university (department, division, college) administration. It is these individuals, surely not as knowledgeable about research and writing as those who engage heavily in it, who often control the needed resources for those who in fact do the work. We have only rarely met a dean or vice president who has written a book, but we have never met an upper-level university administrator who did not express firm views about faculty development and productivity.

Rewards of Writing

If academic writing requires so much time, seldom seems easy to accomplish, intrudes on more desirable activities, and leads many to experience frustration and anger, why do it?

Aside from career advancement opportunities, the truth for many writers is simply that they enjoy it. Personal enjoyment, however, is a multifaceted concept composed of short- and long-term goal acquisition, needs for success, internal and external praise, recognition, satisfaction, and a host of other personal values. Hoover (1980) characterizes the value of professional writing in several ways. The first is to assure employment stability, enhance promotion opportunities, and achieve merit salary increases in publish-or-perish environments. Second, writing provides a method of keeping current with the literature and latest developments in the field. Third, writing provides opportunities for financial rewards outside of one's employment such as book royalties, paid speaking engagements, and increased business referrals. Fourth, writers may be rewarded for their efforts with awards and other peer-generated expressions of professional status and prestige. Finally, writing that results in publication probably enhances the author's self-worth. Hosford (1990) adds unique dimensions to the rewards of writing by noting that age is no barrier and illness seldom poses impediment. Books particularly last beyond a writer's lifetime — a sort of immortality.

For many authors writing serves as a creative outlet. To begin with a blank sheet of paper, an unanswered question, or a vague concept, and end with a manuscript that weaves an elaborate tapestry of words that communicates to others is a gratifying personal experience. Scholarly writing is a creative process likened by some to painting, sculpting, building, or inventing; each yields tangible products designed to enrich their creators and others. In many ways, the developmental process involved in writing is one of professional self-actualization.

The concept of professional self-actualization is shown in Figure 2.3. Academic professionals gain self-esteem over time with the more frequent publication of their manuscripts. Much in the same manner that acquiring tenure frees individuals to examine their self-directed courses of inquiry, academic writing and publishing allow authors to disseminate their ideas and knowledge to bigger audiences. Scholarly

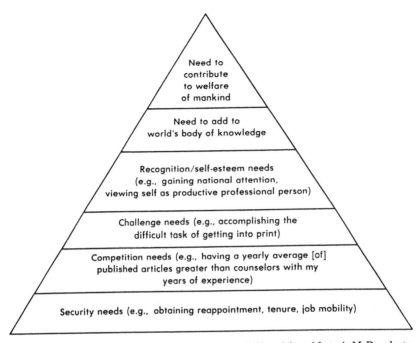

Figure 2.3. Professional and self-fulfillment through publishing. Adapted from A. M. Dougherty. 1982. The publishing counselor. *School Counselor* 30(2): 133–37. Copyright American Association for Counseling and Development. Reprinted with permission.

publishing accomplishments provide increased opportunities for authors to work more closely with leaders, as well as to become leaders in their own right. Such recognition provides opportunities for accumulating indirect benefits as well. For example, Alley and Cargill (1986) note that scholarly publication can lead to recreation and travel, alternative activities to otherwise boring work routines, greater autonomy over work environments, and retirement enhancement.

Returning briefly to the financial rewards of writing, Fulton and Trow (1974, p. 67) suggest "there can be no question that it is research (e.g., writing) which is rewarded by the salary and promotion structures of universities, especially high quality ones." Furthermore, the literature about writing is clear that academics who write receive above average salaries (Hoyt 1974). Katz, Kapes, and Zirkel (1980) reveal a study that assessed professorial salary increases related to publications as $18 for a general article, $102 for an excellent article, and $230 for a book. Another study found an article to be worth between $344 and $395 in salary raises through promotions for faculty authors, compared to their similarly ranked peers without publication accomplishments (Katz, Kapes, and Zirkel 1980). These figures do not account for royalties, increased fees for presentations, board memberships, awards, and other forms of recognition acquired through academic writing.

Fortunately academic writers accrue benefits indirectly from their publications. Van Til (1986), citing a 1981 Columbia University Study of American Authors survey of 2,239 writers, found that only 28 percent earned $20,000 or more and only 10 percent over $45,000. Of the writers surveyed, almost 50 percent had full-time jobs in other fields, 36 percent in universities and 11 percent in publishing.

We have seen, and the research seems to substantiate our observations, that in one area academia seems to differ from other fields — that of job mobility. Whether this is because research and writing are resource bound, time connected, or require long-term cognitive stability, the literature suggests that "institutional mobility can disrupt rather than advance careers" (Rosenfeld and Jones 1986, p. 223). The fortunate exception to this of course may be those occasions wherein a well-known researcher/publisher is "bought" to provide status, eminence, or simply competence for a new or dwindling program. Despite this notable exception it appears that moving from place to place, except early in one's career, is detrimental in the long run.

3

The Basics of Getting Started

Becoming a proficient, efficient, and effective writer requires more than simply writing a lot. It requires both self-control and control of one's immediate environment. No one presumably likes to "work in the dark." Yet, one's surroundings often affect the degree to which tasks are made difficult or easy to accomplish, punishing or rewarding during the process, likely or not to be tried again. This chapter helps set the stage for the writing process by addressing its controllable environmental aspects.

Take a moment to recall the exact location where most of your writing is performed. Many authors need quiet places in which to write, while others seem unaffected by distracting, annoying, or intolerable sights and sounds around them. Next, think about the tools and aids you use when writing. These may include a typewriter or a personal computer, writing tablet, pens or pencils, tape recorder, a comfortable chair, fluorescent lamp or natural sunlight, reference books and journals, and so forth. The point here is to place yourself in a situation that allows you to write as comfortably and expeditiously as possible. In order to help readers to accomplish these objectives, this chapter makes suggestions about writing tools and self-management.

Writing Tools, Aids, and Costs

Not every writer uses the same tools nor has the same priority for their use. Indeed, there are some tools many writers consider

WRITING TOOLS	REQUIRED	DESIRED	HAVE	COST	PRIORITY
1. Comfortable chair					
2. Desk					
3. Desk lamp					
4. File cabinet					
5. Storage folders					
6. Pencils					
7. Pens					
8. Nylon/felt-tipped markers					
9. Pencil/pen holder					
10. Calendar					
11. Paper clips					
12. Stapler/staples					
13. Loose-leaf binders					
14. Bookcase					
15. Dictionary					
16. Thesaurus					
17. Reference books					
18. Journals					
19. Coffee pot and cup					
20. Secluded room					
21. Calculator					
22. Legal-size writing tablet					
23. Regular-size writing tablet					
24. Scratch pad					
25. Typing paper					
26. Copier paper					
27. Typewriter ribbon/cartridge					
28. Printer ribbon/cartridge					
29. Copier ink/toner					
30. Typewriter correction ribbon					
31. Plotter pens					
32. Erasers					
33. Manual typewriter					
34. Electric typewriter					
35. Dictaphone					
36. Tape recorder					
37. Personal computer					
38. Computer printer					
39. Computer plotter					
40. Copier					
41. Computer programs: words					
42. Computer programs: graphs					
43. Computer programs: stats					
44. Computer programs: data					
OTHER ITEMS					
45. _____					
46. _____					
47. _____					

Table 3.1. Priority inventory of writing tools, aids, and costs.

indispensable that others regard as mere conveniences. It is costly to write in terms of time, money, and effort, and personal sacrifices must be made if success is to be achieved regularly (Sikula 1979). Writers usually need a comfortable work area and pleasant surroundings. Additionally, the necessary writing equipment and personal reference materials are often expensive, and the need for these must be prioritized.

It is crucial at this point to put a price tag on each item identified. Obviously, this brings reality and wishful thinking into contact. The next step is to reevaluate the priority listing of needed tools and writing aids with respect to their individual and collective costs. Once prioritized, taking into consideration essentiality and cost, the next step is to identify all tools and aids you currently have or to which you have access. Once this inventory is finished, reassess the priority of items you still need. These steps may eliminate or reduce substantial set-up costs for novice writers. Finally, purchase the remaining items needed, highest priority first. Table 3.1 offers an easy-to-use format for prioritizing writing and work area needs.

Self-Management

Getting started is the hardest part of writing for many people. It is not uncommon to hear novices remark that their lack of writing is a function of "too much work and not enough time" to pursue such interests. These reasons, complaints, or excuses are, in a word, nonsense. Indeed, every adult finds time (or more accurately, makes time) to pursue his or her interests. This section identifies steps leading to effective time management for writing purposes.

Time management is really self-management. It is a technique that must be mastered by academic writers who wish to succeed in publishing. Two important ingredients are deciding how to allocate time and having enough time to do the job (Sorcinelli 1985, p. 1). The first ingredient refers to budgeting time by allotting amounts for certain activities. The second involves managing time by arranging activities, circumstances, and materials as efficiently as possible.

Budgeting Time

Among the first questions to be asked when allocating time for projects is: What do I want to do? However simplistic this question appears to be, answering it is the critical first step. In many ways, this question is synonymous with defining the goal to be accomplished. Once the initial project (goal) is known, it is followed by identifying the activities required to achieve it. These steps are similar to a list of objectives. For example, the initial goal may be to write a paper about outplacement services for displaced workers. The objectives to achieving this goal may consist of performing literature searches, reading information about labor force reductions, taking notes, outlining the topic, writing manuscript drafts, and proofreading.

Obviously each step requires time to complete, which leads to the next task — estimating the amount of time it will take to complete each activity. Once time has been estimated, we suggest novice writers multiply the amount by four to more closely approximate the amount of time really needed to complete a writing project. With experience in writing and time management, perhaps the amount of time actually needed to complete a manuscript will only take twice as long as initially estimated.

Time Management

In order to manage time effectively, the writer should begin with a plan. Such an effort is evident by the goals and objectives exercise mentioned above. Effective time management involves literally making time for an activity by planning and organizing materials and surroundings as much as possible without disrupting respective "schedules." This may seem idealistic to many people, but it is really much easier when several "tricks" are practiced and remembered:

1. Decide what you want to do.
2. Take a few moments to develop a rough outline (goals and objectives).
3. Identify the activities you need to complete to accomplish the tasks.
4. Estimate the amount of time needed to complete each task (remembering to multiply the amount of time by four).
5. Determine whether the project also can be used to fulfill other obligations (such as a term paper or work report).
6. Mark times on your weekly calendar to work on the tasks that do not interfere with other responsibilities.
7. Look at your work environment. Do you have the basic materials to start? Is your work area arranged to economize

retrieval of materials? How much can you do yourself? How much relies on the time and efforts of others?

8. Remember, the project you are working on will not be completed in one sitting. Work on it as time permits, but remember, your use of time can be controlled.

Additional Hints and Cautions

Time Wasters and Time Consumers

A variety of "time wasters" appear with great regularity. Procrastination, distractions, and inefficiency top the list. Internal and external sources of tension and stress also contribute to lost time. In addition to "time wasters" are "time consumers." Family activities, employment, transportation to and from work, waiting in lines, leisure and recreation, eating and sleeping, socializing, and home and community service are a few of the many activities in which people participate daily. "Time consumers" indeed are the composite activities of daily living. "Time wasters," on the other hand, can be found within such activities or can be used to reduce the quantity and quality of activities people encounter daily. However unfortunate the occurrence of "time wasters" is, it is more so when people allow themselves to "waste" their own time.

Creativity

Time may be lost in unproductive activities, but seldom is it lost when used for creative endeavors. Writing requires creativity, something that can be neither planned nor arbitrarily sandwiched into one's daily schedule. Usually creativity requires time and reflection to develop and mature. Often creative ideas seem to occur at random, and seldom during the times set aside for "being creative." Because of this, efficient writers have learned to plan ahead by jotting down notes when such creative thoughts occur. Later, the notes can be retrieved as reminders during time set aside for writing (Alley and Cargill 1986). Relying on note taking does have its problems. First, take enough time to write notes that you will understand at a subsequent reading. Second, place notes where you won't forget them when they are needed. Third, don't forget you have notes.

Personal Computers

One of the most significant advances for writers is affordable microcomputers and word-processing programs. "Computers can help beginning writers learn to revise their initial drafts with less emphasis on lexical substitution and grammatical correctness and with more emphasis on progressive reshaping of ideas through successive drafts" (Bean 1983, p. 146). Computers economize the time required to rearrange words, sentences, paragraphs, and sections of papers from one draft to another. Computer-assisted printers enable writers to assemble multiple originals of the same paper. What results often is higher quality work and about four times the productivity of handwritten or conventionally typed papers (Mullins 1982). Moreover, computers enable writers to "find, replace, delete, insert and move words, center titles, number pages, count words, create indexes," check spelling, structure references in correct formats, include tables/figures/graphs, and, with laser printing, turn out commercial-quality copies (Bali 1984, p. 6).

The "magic" of computers and computer-assisted printers, however, is not always the panacea computer enthusiasts would have everyone believe. While basic personal computers, printers, and word-processing programs have become much more affordable, their cost is still much higher than a standard manual or electric typewriter. Additionally, the time saved by a computer to make changes to a paper and print multiple originals may be offset by a slow printer, a slow microprocessing unit in the computer, and/or a word-processing program that is insufficient for the task at hand. Similarly, it takes time to become proficient enough to use the processing program to create papers. Although computer literacy will become essential for most every professional in the future, one should consider several factors before adopting such a system.

1. How much can you afford to spend for a computer and printer?
2. How much memory do you want or think you will need in the computer?
3. How many floppy disk drives do you want in the computer?
4. Do you want floppy drives that accommodate 5.25- or 3.50-inch diskettes or both?

5. Do you want a hard disk drive in your computer and if so, how much memory do you want it to have?
6. What speed of a processor do you want in the computer?
7. Do you want a lap-top computer or a desk-top model?
8. Do you want an IBM-compatible model or an Apple system?
9. Should your printer be dot matrix, laser, or have a daisy wheel?
10. How fast must the printer be?
11. Do you want an increased memory buffer in the printer?
12. Do you want a dot-matrix printer that is capable of printing letter-quality materials?
13. Do you need a printer with a carriage large enough for spreadsheets?
14. Should the printer be capable of printing graphs or do you want to purchase a plotter as well?
15. Do you want a computer with a built-in printer?
16. Do you want word-processing programs that are compatible with the ones used by your colleagues?
17. Do you want an integrated computer program (one that combines word processing, graphics, data management, spelling, and merging)?
18. Do you want a modem to communicate with other computers and printers by telephone?
19. How frequently will you use the computer and printer?

Some writing activities can be performed more efficiently when computers are used for word-processing purposes. Before investing in state-of-the-art tools that are intended to increase writing productivity, it is important to assess their capabilities in relation to your needs.

4

Writing Can Be Fun, But Seldom Is It Easy

Ask yourself a simple question, "What activities do I do for fun that are considered work by others?" Next, ask yourself a more difficult question, "Why do I enjoy these activities when they are laborious for others?" Your answer to the second question may include affirmations of personal values, skills, abilities, and interests. It could also include personality characteristics such as motivation, need for accomplishment, need for recognition, and feelings of self-esteem and confidence.

Everyone has encountered people who make what they do appear to be so easy and simple that anyone could accomplish the same thing. Then we try the same activity only to discover how much skill is required to master the task at the level of proficiency demonstrated by those we observed. The ability to write publishable papers requires mastery of skills in much the same way. Motivation is essential, practice is critical, and developing a writing habit is crucial. Six topics are discussed in this chapter that examine aspects of successful publication. These include: (1) taking chances, (2) developing writing habits, (3) noting the price of motivation and practice, (4) avoiding common mistakes, (5) doing your homework, and (6) collaborating with others.

Take a Chance

Persistence and Patience

Any profession carries with it obligations to communicate ideas and new discoveries to colleagues. The academic community embraces such an obligation among its heterogenous faculty members; however, unlike most other work settings, academia conveys this obligation through its faculty to those in its charge — students, the current protégés who will become role models and mentors for others. If one assumes that an instructor's enthusiasm about a course subject facilitates student learning, what impression might be communicated about writing for publication by faculty who resist doing it?

Writing takes time and effort like most other activities. Those who invest in it do not enjoy having their efforts criticized or rejected by others. When one considers that 60 to 90 percent of all article manuscripts are rejected (Dorn 1985a; Gladding 1984; Watkins 1982) and only 5 percent of book proposals ever result in contracts offered by publishers (Robinson and Higbee 1978), it is not easy for novice writers to avoid feelings of failure and low self-confidence that such outcomes produce (Johnson 1982). Improving one's writing skills and increasing publication rates may be aided, however, by understanding several important points:

1. Few article manuscripts are accepted without revision.
2. Every book manuscript will require revision before being published.
3. Published manuscripts are read by people with varied backgrounds. Your article or book must communicate its information clearly, succinctly, and accurately.
4. Try to separate your ego from the manuscript. Editorial criticisms address areas needing improvement in the paper, not the writer.
5. Try to follow the advice and guidance offered by editors and reviewers. Their comments can be your greatest aid to achieving publishing success.
6. Think of unaccepted manuscripts in terms of "returns" gained through practice instead of rejection (Penaskovic 1985).
7. You have nothing to lose and everything to gain when submitting a manuscript — it may be accepted the first time.
8. If you are not satisfied with the feedback from the initial publisher, try sending the manuscript to another. It is very

August 25, 1988

Dear Ralph,

I thought I'd write you this letter "of discovery" which is related to your manuscript on publishing. You quote Tryon's article about getting published and her effort to "track" the history of her 31 articles. That got me to wondering about my own stuff, so here is what I found.

I started "professional" publishing in 1964. The pubs include articles, monographs, reports, books, etc. I decided to only review the articles.

DISCOVERY NO.1:
    35 articles were juried. 9 were not juried.
    Of the 35 juried articles, 4 were invited.
    Of the 35, invited or not, 32 required some change or corrections on the manuscript.
DISCOVERY IMPLICATIONS:
    This means that for your manuscript you many want to emphasize that corrections and changes are a part of the publishing routine.
DISCOVERY NO. 2:
    I looked over the 31 juried articles that were not invited in order to see how many tries it took to get published. In other words, how many journals had a chance to reject me. The left column contains the number of tries. The column on the right is the number or articles per try. In other words, it took me 4 times to get 3 articles published.

Tries	Journals
1	24
2	2
3	2
4	3

DISCOVERY IMPLICATIONS
    First, don't give up. You may have to change your material or your style or get some advice, but don't give up. Second, know your journals. Some of my early failures were based on poor knowledge on my part. But, some of the early failures were also due to the fact that I didn't want to send manuscript after manuscript to the same journal. What I did find out was that the journal could stock you if you agreed to publish in that journal at a once a year rate.
DISCOVERY NO. 3:
    How long did it take to be approved for publishing; the "in press" magic. The column on the left is the number of months from the time the journal first acknowledged my manuscript to the time that it said "Wow, super duper, you are in our ranks." The column on the right is the number of juried articles that made the ranks.

Months	Articles
1–4	14
5–8	7
9–12	3
13–16	6

    P.S. This chart only reflects the number of months between the first letter and the acceptance letter. It does not reflect when the article was finally PUBLISHED.
DISCOVERY IMPLICATIONS:
    Once you put that manuscript in the mail, go on to the next one. Don't sit around waiting for the mail person with the letter from the journal. Need I say more?

I hope some of these "findings" are interesting or of use to you. Gee, I found all kinds of interesting stuff about me that I had forgotten. (Mmmm, I wonder if I should look at my dissertation.)

    Best Wishes,
    Chuck K.

Figure 4.1. Letter from Chuck Kokaska.

important, however, that you inform the first editor of your intention to withdraw the manuscript from further consideration in that publication before submitting it elsewhere. Failure to do so often is considered unethical.

Tryon (1986) wrote an excellent article about manuscript acceptance. Over an eight-year period, she kept track of thirty-one articles she authored or coauthored. Only three manuscripts were accepted without need for revision, while nine manuscripts were accepted after revisions were made and nineteen rejected by the initial journal to which they were sent. Of the rejections, all but two were accepted and published later by other editors! Although twenty-nine publications in eight years is a considerable accomplishment, Tryon's persistence and patience are the message for beginning writers to remember.

Chuck Kokaska, coordinator of the Special Education Program at California State University, Long Beach, who reviewed and provided feedback for this book, noted Tryon's follow-up on her publications. Out of curiosity he examined his own log of published articles and then shared his findings with the authors. His letter "of discovery" (Figure 4.1), which records his professional articles, does not examine the time records of his books, monographs, and reports, but it does provide some very salient observations about professional publishing.

Talent Versus Discipline

"Talent can and must be developed through study and practice, it can't be taught" (Holmes 1982, p. 9). As mentioned above, some people seem to be born with more talent than others. Genetic endowment, however, is not the issue. There is little doubt that those involved in academic writing have the experience and often the education necessary to select and use words appropriately. Like many others, Holmes believes that talent emerges from a strong belief in one's own ability to succeed coupled with persistence, patience, and self-discipline.

Dorn (1985b), echoing Holmes' views, states that those "with a minimum of raw talent . . . [and the] desire to write for publication, must be dedicated, disciplined, and determined" (pp. 512–13). In this context, dedication refers to being deeply involved in and staying current with the latest developments in one's field and in its literature.

Discipline simply relates to the constant effort that is required, namely, making writing a habit. The best academic authors, even those who do not write every day, are always doing something applicable to the process — discovery, production, note taking, learning — on a daily basis. Determination requires resiliency, an ability to learn from criticism in order to achieve success.

Developing Writing Habits

Alley and Cargill (1986) identify four requirements necessary to become an accomplished academic author:

1. Peruse the field, particularly the relevant literature, to analyze and determine your place in its scheme.
2. Practice your communication abilities, especially writing skills, at every opportunity.
3. Persist with writing efforts directed for publication despite initial obstacles such as rejections or demands for revision.
4. Shape your writing skills with information acquired from practice and past experiences.

Psychological Approaches

One of the most prolific authorities on the subject of psychological approaches to writing is Robert Boice of California State University, Long Beach. During a brief presentation to a group of faculty participants in a mentoring study, Boice (1987b) offered the following outline:

A. Traditional Strategies for Facilitating Writing and Treating Writing Blocks (listed in evolutionary sequence)
   1. Automacity
      - establishes momentum
      - permits starting regardless of mood, readiness, or motivation
      - generates useful prose
      - generates ideas for writing
      - cures for impatience

2. External controls
   - contingency management ensures regular, productive output
   - arrangement of nondistracting conditions for writing
   - scheduling of writing in terms of specific, finishable subtasks
   - social contracts for meeting regularly to write
3. Cognitive and emotional reeducation
   - attempts to correct myths about writing ("good writing must be spontaneous, original/novel/significant, and fast")
   - talking aloud protocols used to observe "poor vs. good" writers reveal important differences in areas including time spent prewriting
   - cognitive researchers train problem writers to recognize and then modify their negative self-talk and emotions before and during writing by substituting "psych-up" statements and relaxation
4. Training the social skills of writing
   - helping writers make writing a more public and publicly acceptable activity
   - building social, cultural, and collaborative supports for writing
   - helping writers cope with the editorial process
   - sharing imperfect drafts and letting others do some of the work

B. Nontraditional, Superordinate Writing Facilitators
   1. Regular writing practice
   2. Writing in brief, daily sessions amidst busy schedules
      - disadvantages of writing "binges" include procrastination, writing with fatigue and without revision, lengthy warm-up time — research evidence shows that brief, daily writing sessions produce more output, quality/creativity, success, and satisfaction than does binge writing
      - research shows that usual claims of being too busy for writing are untrue

- research shows that times set aside for binge writing usually result in meeting few intended goals for writing
3. Continued social prods provide advice and support for writers struggling to establish new habits and confidence
C. Most Common Profile of Problem Writers
1. Combined pattern: High scores on indolent-idealess items
2. Combined pattern: High scores on pessimistic-fearful-depression — includes phobic tendencies and rigid rules about writing
3. Single pattern: High scores on elitism — includes perfectionism and beliefs that most writing by others is subpar and useless
4. Combined pattern: High scores on procrastination-impatience — describes writers who actively seek external, aversive pressures to make them write, and once writing, proceed impatiently
D. Summary of What Makes Writing Easier
1. Incorporate all traditional treatment strategies
2. Regular practice in brief sessions, during daily busywork, before feeling ready
3. Cultural supports including nonlocal contacts
4. Exercises in facilitative writing skills
   - modeling successful writing styles
   - building a greater store of ideas through note taking
   - practicing ready alternatives between composing and editing
   - crafting keener observational skills including a sense of audience
   - generating writing materials while juxtaposing modalities (auditory, visual, factual, olfactory)
   - writing on word processors and with the aid of software that regenerates organizational approaches, spelling checks, etc.

Practical Essentials

O'Brien and Johnson (1980) suggest writers follow the "discovery-production-publication-dissemination" sequence. The four steps are:
1. Identify the subject matter (What do you want to say?).
2. Decide on appropriate outlets (journals, publishers).
3. Develop the manuscript (content, format, appearance).
4. Profit from reviews (Use comments to enrich and revise.).

Expanding on the above, Cappeto and Kauffman (1983) suggest that writers initially determine what it is they wish to write. Because composition is a rigorous task, having a definite idea of the reasons, purposes, and coverage of a manuscript will serve as an excellent starting place. Next, you should determine the audience for the finished product. This answer will influence not only what is said, but also how it is said. Third, select the best potential outlet for the manuscript. You should become familiar with the type of articles published by journals or the style and range of books produced by publishers. Taking time to learn about potential publishing outlets will provide writing models for your own efforts. Finally, note reviewers' comments and editors' suggestions. You may not always agree with them, but more often than not, you will learn a great deal. Many reviewers, for example, will delete unnecessary verbiage or point out recurring and annoying phraseology. Try reading their "revised" copy thoroughly before rejecting their suggestions. Frequently you will find that their comments make your manuscript much easier to read.

The Price of Motivation and Practice

The hints mentioned thus far have a price. Hosford (1990) calls the necessity for self-discipline "giving up fun time" (p. 11). As previously noted it is costly to write, costly in terms of money, effort, time, and personal sacrifices if you intend to succeed (Sikula 1979). "Paying the price," devoting your time, also involves going to conventions (frequently at one's own expense) to look at recent publication displays and to talk with publishers' representatives. Personal contacts made at conventions, writing workshops, and professional meetings with editors, publishers, reviewers, and other writers often are worth the extra effort and expense.

For many the most costly aspect of writing for publications involves time away from your spouse and children. Sikula (1979) points out that many successful writers have paid dearly for spending long hours writing and being away from their families. However heartless it may seem, the time invested in writing is a matter of setting priorities. Those concerned with professional advancement, writing, and making contributions to academic literature, and who in fact have substantial publishing records, often have strong, supportive spouses and families or none at all. Writing is not a family project, although many spouses review and critique work (Sikula 1979, p. 99). There is at least some family sacrifice in one form or another associated with extended publication records.

The motivation behind most academicians with publishing accomplishments is not monetary. The most common motivators involve career advancement and the desire to contribute to the knowledge in a chosen field (Sikula 1979). Few academicians really make money as a result of their publications. In fact, if one considers the time, effort, and money invested to develop a respectable manuscript, most people would agree that there is little if any financial reward. It is much more likely to cost money than to produce it.

Other considerations should be mentioned that involve paying the price. Many publishers today, for example, require authors to at least partially subsidize publication costs (Luey 1989; Sikula 1979). This practice, which once was rare and frowned upon, is now much more acceptable and is engaged in frequently by beginners who often are willing to pay for their manuscripts to be printed. Scholars who are uncomfortable with this practice should realize, however, that this is regularly done in other professions.

It is not uncommon, also, for contributors to a publication to be asked to join the sponsoring association, to subscribe to the publication, or perhaps to buy or guarantee the sale of a certain number of copies of a finished product. In addition, many of the most prestigious journals require authors to pay a set amount per page for articles accepted and printed (Sikula 1979). To do so is perfectly professional and many times absolutely essential to finance the publication.

Finally, there is one last cost associated with getting manuscripts into print and establishing a publication record. Authors need to acquire extra copies of books or articles when they are printed. These should be for friends, relatives, immediate supervisors, and for future use in dossier preparation, job hunting, and for providing reprints upon request. Over time purchasing reprints becomes difficult, if not impossible.

Common Mistakes to Avoid

Sikula (1979) identifies twelve common mistakes made by academic writers.

1. Often manuscripts seem to be written with no apparent purpose. To avoid undue reader aggravation, state the purpose of a work explicitly at the beginning. Your purpose should never be implied, assumed, or hidden.
2. Academic works often omit basic information. Avoid this mistake by organizing facts, involving who, what, where, when, and how.
3. Writers can avoid mistakes by carefully checking sources and making clear distinctions between opinion and fact.
4. Many authors overgeneralize, oversimplify, or assume cause-and-effect relationships beyond those which their data support. To avoid these sure signs of lack of sophistication in and understanding of sound writing and academic principles, make certain that independent and dependent variables are clearly related.
5. Some writers are so cautious about how they present their results or conclusions that they have nothing new or creative to report.
6. Recognize that absolute objectivity is impossible. In order to avoid ambiguity and leaving readers to derive their own conclusions about the topic of your manuscript, take a position and defend it. Do not be afraid to interpret data keeping in mind that your own biases and values will influence your interpretation.

7. Authors often use words incorrectly. Many writers try to impress readers by using bandwagon terms, jargon, and big, fancy words. Plain talk is especially appropriate when your audience has a high proportion of lay readers. Avoid using words that you do not fully understand, as well as words and phrases that have a unique colloquial interpretation.

8. Accurate and thorough documentation of ideas and works of others appears to be becoming less frequent in the literature. Crediting the ideas of others demonstrates academic integrity and familiarity with the field.

9. Sometimes articles are so uninteresting that their information goes unused. To help increase appeal, use examples, analogies, anecdotes, and illustrations to add meaning and relevance to your message.

10. Avoid redundancy. Keep manuscripts as concise and parsimonious as possible without sacrificing substantive content.

11. Nearly every publisher and journal adopt a standardized writing format and style. For whatever reasons, however, many authors use individual writing styles and formats that frequently are difficult to follow. To avoid this, use the style manual recommended by the journal/publisher, vary your sentence structure, choose verbs and adjectives carefully, be consistent in punctuation, use active rather than passive voice whenever possible, and use the standard rules of spelling, grammar, writing, and documentation.

12. Proofread diligently. Most writers do not seem to follow this simple rule based on the number of typographical errors, misspellings, and incomplete sentences often found in reviewed manuscripts.

In addition to these items, Watkins (1982) offers seven points of "journal etiquette" that writers learn over time. Beginning writers who take time to follow these points early in their careers are a breath of fresh air to editors and reviewers alike.

1. Follow the format and guidelines adopted by the publisher.
2. Make your writing relevant to the readership.
3. Present novel ideas or new applications of "old" information.
4. Be interested in and solicitous of feedback.
5. Be concise, scrutinizing, and parsimonious.
6. Be neat. Type your manuscript on bond paper (at least 20 percent cotton rag), avoid smudges and handwritten inserted corrections, establish margins on all sides of each page (and don't exceed them to squeeze in an extra few letters of a word), and use camera-ready tables, figures, and illustrations if possible.
7. Be patient and willing to revise as recommended.

Doing Your Homework

In publishing, as in life, there is nothing more important to success than thorough preparation. Mistakes, both big and small, can and should be avoided. How can mistakes be minimized? How can one adequately prepare? How can the probability of success be increased? The answer is relatively simple, and one which people have heard since first entering school — do your homework.

Sikula (1979) tells you how.

First, take the time to become familiar with the journal or publishing company to whom you are submitting a manuscript in order to avoid wasting time and effort (Fine 1987). Acquaint yourself with the readership, format requirements, numbers of copies requested, and proper mailing address for manuscript receipt. Submit everything requested, such as biographical sketch(es), return postage, self-addressed envelopes, and camera-ready art. Do not expect a prompt or favorable response to your work if you have not paid attention to the basic submission requirements.

Second, keep in mind that publishable materials have two elements: something of substance to say and style. Send your manuscripts to publishers who have demonstrated interest in the type of material being submitted. Some publishers want short, concise, descriptive works, while others desire lengthy, extended analyses or data interpretations.

47

Third, determine whether the journal or publishing company to whom you intend to submit manuscripts is accepting them. This can be accomplished by a letter or a phone call. Not only will such an inquiry save you time and effort if a sizable backlog of accepted papers exists, it provides an opportunity to initiate a personal contact with those whom you will become associated in publishing circles in the future.

Fourth, spend several hours in your local library leafing through local, state, regional, and national journals and other publications sponsored by your field and by public agencies. Many publications discovered in this way are of high quality and probably are more in need of material than some of the most popular and nationally known publications.

Fifth, submit only complete manuscripts in a final, polished form. There are few exceptions to this rule of thumb, especially for beginning writers. Only well-established and known authors with demonstrated writing abilities usually are allowed to provide only outlines or a sample of their final product.

Sixth, it is counterproductive to submit anything other than your best effort. Although the chances of acceptance are usually low, if accepted because of an "in" with a publisher or for some other reason, then once in print this becomes a permanent reflection of the quality of your scholarship. A poorly written or weak publication is often worse than no publication at all.

Seventh, organization and planning are essential. There are very few shortcuts to publishing success. Hard work, effort, and a great deal of time and care are required. Professional writers do not simply sit down and start typing pages of finished material. They think, outline, research, organize, reorganize, and usually spend much more time preparing to write and revising than actually writing. It is not uncommon, for example, for book authors to organize materials for years before writing the manuscript.

Finally, inadequate preparation usually is obvious when the final product is revealed. Adequate preparation is more than half the battle; the execution of the skills is generally fun and often rewarding. Sloppy manuscripts, misspelled words, and grammatical and typographical errors are distracting and must be avoided (Gay and Edgil 1989; Smith 1988). Requests made by publishers and editors for specific revisions and deadlines should be met. By doing your homework conscientiously, you are enhancing subsequent acceptance of your work and establishing a professional reputation among your peers.

Collaborative Assistance

More and more frequently "fewer single-authored articles are being accepted for publication" (Gladding 1984, p. 630). One explanation for this is that novice writers "seek help of a colleague who is already an accomplished writer" (Hoover 1980, p. 352). Other reasons supported by research suggest that many writers maintain their momentum and enthusiasm longer when working with others (Johnson 1982) and express a strong need for collegiality and opportunities to interact or gain support from peers (Sorcinelli 1985). Some research (Jones, Preusz, and Finkelstein 1989) has even indicated that those who utilize colleagues in conducting research "demonstrate a fourfold increase in career number of publications" over those who do not collaborate (p. 643). For those with little or no published writing experience, collaboration with an accomplished senior author serves as a learning experience. One often hears "the easiest way to hook into the publishing network is to find a mentor" (Conciatore 1990, p. 3). Unfortunately, not all learning experiences have positive effects. This is true of collaborative writing as well.

Numerous benefits accrue from collaboration, not least of which is the synergism that often arises between coauthors (Buddemeier 1981). Coauthoring an article with an established writer is an excellent way to begin and continue a record of publishing accomplishments. Writing with others also leads to expanding one's network among peers and colleagues, gaining new ideas and interests, and developing mentoring possibilities (Gladding 1984). Increased publication productivity is an obvious outcome of successful collaborative efforts.

We have both worked with a large number of junior professionals, master's students, doctoral students, and assistant professors. This collaboration with novice writers, although very time-consuming for the more experienced and efficient author, is exceptionally helpful for the new writer. Our experience indicates that sometime after the third or fourth successful collaborative work new writers suddenly begin to understand the degree to which the experienced professor "carried" them for the first few publications. Many times then the junior will take a senior role in yet other publications partially as a way of expressing gratitude and partially as a demonstration of newly achieved skills.

There are several other aspects we feel should be mentioned. The first is that for a variety of reasons to be examined below, we decided to work only once with an aspiring writer. Although this collaboration was successful, the psychological or interpersonal requirements were not present for further desirable interaction. The person was simply too difficult to get along with, feeling that after just a few articles that he had all the answers to all questions about academic writing. The second factor, also to be examined further, involves time and commitment. We have found we simply cannot work with everyone who asks. One of us has not originated a study, a research project, or a publication in over two years. All the time available has been consumed by contract books, solicited articles, and requests for collaboration from both new and experienced colleagues. Far more projects are politely turned down than are ever started. New academics should realize they, and many others, are asking to work with a published professor for the same reason — a well-documented track record. One does not attain such a record by frequently stepping off the track. Given these reasons "graduate students should keep in mind that highly productive faculty members do not necessarily make the best mentors" (Cox and Blount 1989, p. 736).

Another part of collaboration with a beginner involves time and effort. We have constantly heard and observed that the novice to academic writing and publishing spends a far greater ratio of time per successful acceptance. That is to say it takes the less skilled more time to produce an acceptable manuscript. Unfortunately many people equate time and effort with quality. "I worked real hard on this . . . it has taken weeks . . . I spent many hours . . ." are refrains that perhaps subtly penalize efficiency and skill. More than once we have spent just a few days totally rewriting a manuscript that took months to produce. Likely this rewrite ability comes from years of reviewing term papers, research papers, theses, dissertations, and judging manuscripts on professional journal boards. The recipient of the rewritten journal manuscript may or may not be able to determine what suddenly makes the paper publishable. Those who do see and understand are likely to enter further collaborative efforts. Those who do not are likely to receive their feedback directly from a journal editor on their next noncollaborative work. Junior collaborators especially should remember that we do not pay a physician or lawyer an outrageous sum for one hour of their time, but instead for the education and experience that they bring to bear in that one hour.

There are many potential pitfalls associated with collaborative efforts. Although the list seems long, initial awareness may help reduce or eliminate many areas of concern before they become problems. Table 4.1 provides an overview of issues that coauthors must resolve early in their collaborative efforts. Failing to establish mutual agreement may lead some writers to avoid collaboration in the future. That would be a mistake.

One of the most seemingly innocuous yet volatile issues that plagues collaborative efforts in academia involves the order in which authors are listed on the title page once a manuscript is finished. Few competent and accomplished writers have not encountered this conflict during their careers. Students in particular frequently are abused in this regard. In part, the problem derives from misplaced goodwill, lack of preparation and awareness among authors, varying ethical standards of professional associations, and internal policies of employing organizations and agencies. Tryon (1981), for example, found that when "men and women published together, men held first authorship significantly more often than women, which suggests that they initiated the research. . . . Where one man published with one woman [however] . . . men and women served as first authors an equal number of times" (p. 186). Sugar and Tracy (1989) feel that it is "naive" to assume that gender is a causative in publication productivity without more evidence to substantiate such a case.

One inference suggested by initiating is that first authorship is a concomitant expectation. That orientation, however, is not the case in many circumstances. One of this book's authors worked once with an individual who contributed no more than 10 to 20 percent to a project. This person claimed frequently, "Where I come from the person that has the idea goes first." He was told that, "Where I come from the person who does the successful work goes first." Others who have examined the ordering of multiple authorship citations conclude that

PROBLEMS	POSSIBLE SOLUTIONS

1. Order of authorship listing (first, second, last)	A. Equally shared
	  1. list alphabetically, or
	  2. designate as a note that authorship is shared equally, or
	  3. agree to alternate listing order if more than one manuscript is planned among the same authors
	B. Traditional listing
	  1. list by the amount of work performed by each author, or
	  2. list by the significance of each author's contribution, or
	  3. list by previously agreed amount of responsibility assigned each author during the project and/or writing.

2. Assigned responsibilities	A. Before starting, decide what needs to be done and who will do what. B. Before starting, decide whether one author will supervise and monitor all aspects of the project and/or writing. C. If one author is designated as "principal investigator" or "senior author" a priori, decide nature and scope of work expected of that position in the project and/or writing.
3. Credit for ideas	A. Before starting, decide whether an "idea" (without substantive follow-up work on the project and/or writing) is sufficient for its originator to be credited with first authorship.
4. Initiating projects/writing	A. Before starting to write, decide whether first authorship will be given to the person who started the project, even when subsequent major work is completed by other collaborators.

Table 4.1. Pitfalls of collaborative authorship.

contribution should "be evaluated by its scholarly importance rather than by the amount of time and energy invested in it" (Bridgwater, Bornstein, and Walkenbach 1981, p. 525). In other words, merit determines citation order instead of personal or professional status, paid versus voluntary work, or supervisor versus subordinate work status. "Colleagues or supervisors should neither ask to have their names on manuscripts nor allow their names to be put on manuscripts reporting research with which they themselves have not been intimately involved" (Day 1988, p. 22).

Minimizing Negative Consequences

In order to avoid the many pitfalls of collaboration found in Table 4.1, Fox and Faver (1982) examined principles and strategies of successful multiple-writer liaisons. Three basic sets of variables emerge that facilitate working together. The first are intellectual variables comprising shared interests, perspectives, skills, and competencies. The second are personal variables consisting of similar or compatible work habits and complementary personalities. Added to these are structural variables such as academic or employment rank/position, sex, and number. Rank refers to whether collaboration is a peer alliance or a junior-senior relationship. Sex refers to avoiding irrelevant and discriminatory sex-role stereotyping. Number refers to the variety of ideas, skills and knowledge, disagreements, ambiguous responsibilities, time delays, and similar issues that can undermine or enhance collaborative relationships.

Fox and Faver (1982) suggest that tasks can be shared, separated, or divided among collaborators depending on: (1) the nature of the tasks, (2) the skill and competence of participants, (3) the time and resources available, and (4) the degree of control each participant desires. Furthermore, these authors recommend that the overall project should be scheduled and an informal contract entered into among the participants. It is this negotiated contract that addresses "the questions of authorship and ordering names for publications" (pp. 335–36).

Although like Fox and Faver we have found a contract to be the best option available, it sometimes is not enough. Recently one of us worked with a group of six faculty members on a very large project. At the end it was found that two did half the work, another professor did a quarter of the project, and for the last quarter no one else produced even one useable page. The problem, of course, was that there was no way to enforce the contract other than to politely beg off any further collaboration with the nonproductive members. As Day (1988) notes, "some workers wheedle or cajole their colleagues so effectively that they become authors of most or all of the papers coming out of their laboratory. . . . the practice is not recommended" (p. 23).

Asking for Help

Almost all writers with publishing records have at least one person to whom they can turn for assistance. In many instances, a spouse or former colleague provides feedback to writers. Sometimes, writers are fortunate to have a secretary or other staff members who proofread and/or provide suggestions about wording and general appearance of manuscripts. Students often seek faculty input when preparing papers, especially if they plan to submit their work for publication. Regardless of who the writer is, however, asking for help involves knowing an imposition is being placed on others. Here are a few things to consider before requesting help:

1. The review of an average manuscript by journal editorial board members takes approximately four to six hours.
2. An adequate review involves such things as criticism, suggestions for improvements, reanalysis, and recommended action.
3. A manuscript generally is sent to a reviewer who shares similar interests with the author.
4. Journal reviewers seldom know the identity of a manuscript's author(s), thus reducing potential biasing or prejudicial assessment of the paper.
5. When asking someone to review your paper, know whether you want a thorough or a casual review (i.e., four-plus hours or thirty minutes).

This list is particularly important for new writers. We know of few universities that have the amount of resources as the CSULB Office of Faculty Development. This division functions specifically to assist new writers and publishers (for teaching and service as well) and is operated by professors with remarkable records of achievement. Because most universities do not have such an excellent resource, potential writers often turn to other sources. In some schools, divisions, or departments it is common to ask colleagues for help. In many settings, however, this may be inappropriate. Often university administrators are charged with faculty development, but as we have illustrated, they may not be the best qualified to comment on a manuscript. We feel that the best thing a new writer can do is ask successful senior authors and promotion/tenure personnel for assistance.

This chapter revealed that publication efforts require practice, patience, perseverance, developing sound writing habits, and following the guidelines of editors and publishers. It also identified common mistakes many novice writers make that sabotage their efforts. Armed with the process mechanics contained in this chapter, readers should be prepared to take their first steps in writing. Chapter 5 examines the least threatening (and perhaps most useful) writing avenue for novice writers to pursue — local publications.

5

In the Beginning There Was Local Copy

Aside from casual conversation with colleagues, what is your most current source of information concerning your occupational interests? If you work for a large government agency or university or are a member of a professional association, chances are you receive such information through newsletters. Although some newsletters may have a staff of hired writers, many do not. Editors often rely on the contributions of unpaid writers who volunteer their time to fill the pages with meaningful information you and your colleagues read. The purpose of this chapter is to acquaint novice writers with one of the least threatening outlets for initial writing efforts. Helpful hints for publishing in newsletters follow sections addressing association and employer periodicals.

Association News

Most professional associations periodically mail newsletters to their members. Newsletters are similar to local newspapers in as much as they provide such things as brief news articles of potential occupational interest, selective product advertisements relevant to an organization's constituency, and job listings. As with community newspapers, their depth and variety of coverage, length, and frequency depend on factors such as sources of revenues, budget allocations, publication costs, and circulation volume. Needless to say, not all newsletters are created equal.

Publication Frequency

Newsletters are the most frequently distributed organizational publications members receive to stay abreast of current events and issues occurring in or affecting their respective fields. As part of an individual's annual membership dues, newsletters might be received as frequently as once a month, but generally not less often than every two months. Delays in receiving current issues may be encountered, however, since most publications of this type are sent by bulk mail either directly from the organization or from a contracted publisher.

Size and Length

Organizational newsletters come in many shapes and sizes. The *Psychiatric Research Report* of the American Psychiatric Association, for example, is printed on heavy paper stock that folds to the size of a standard page (i.e., 8 ½ by 11 inches). The *Guidepost* of the American Association for Counseling and Development, on the other hand, resembles the size and paper quality used by local daily newspapers. While the number of pages contained in any single issue depends on many factors (such as amount of news to report, costs of printing and mailing, and size of an organization), length can vary from four to thirty pages.

Variety of Sources

Organizational newsletters are used to keep subscribing members informed about specific issues and topics related to and consistent with an association's mission. Moreover, it is not uncommon for associations to be comprised of related divisions which may also have regional, state, and/or local chapters. Newsletters often are published at each level of an association and its divisions, from national to local levels. For example, the National Rehabilitation Association is composed of seven divisions at the national level, each of which have state chapters and some local groups as well. If a member belonged to this association and each of its divisions, he or she would receive a minimum of eight newsletters every two months from the national level and the same number at the state level, a total of ninety-six issues received annually (sixteen national and state newsletters six times per year). The number of newsletters published annually by this organization alone provides more than ample opportunity for novice writers to submit articles. Other associations may offer even more writing outlets.

Variety of Coverage

The degree to which newsletters cover a variety of topics depends largely on the size of the respective organizations they represent, operating budget size, number of subscribers, variety of organizational goals, variety of occupational interests represented by members, and networking systems available for gathering additional information. Despite a wide variety of topics covered, basic areas that most news-letters include are a front page feature article, assorted topical specialty articles, a message from the organization president, an editorial, up-coming meetings and conferences, announcements of employment openings and/or positions being sought, letters to the editor, calls for correspondence and address changes among subscribing members, calls for nominations to fill elected positions within the organization, and candidates' campaign statements.

Depth of Coverage

Information reported in newsletters attempts to present essential facts and activities rather than give detailed reviews and interpretative analyses. In this regard, newsletters are written much like newspapers. Photographs generally are incorporated when they add to article content or are considered by the editor to be of interest to the subscribing membership (e.g., convention highlights, noted speakers). Furthermore, the information contained in news articles frequently is assumed to be factual and verifiable. Seldom are footnotes and reference citations printed as part of an article as one might expect to find in journals, books, or other academically oriented publications. Similarly, statistical analyses seldom extend beyond relatively straightforward percentages and dollar values.

Finally, newsletter articles usually are formatted in narrow columns. Sometimes as many as five or six columns appear per page. Because of this method, it is important for writers to use succinct sentence construction. Communicate the point of each sentence effectively by using economical wording and phrasing.

Employer News

Many large employers distribute monthly, weekly, or even daily newsletters to employees. Unlike professional organization newsletters, however, the potential audience is much less numerous and often comprises a heterogenous variety of training, experience, and interests than generally is represented among association members. As a result of this, employer newsletters frequently are no longer than two to four pages, provide information about upcoming social and/or training activities sponsored by the employer or a unit within the company, offer suggestions about leisure/recreational/health events, and communicate schedules of meetings and other business functions.

Because of the diversity of backgrounds of employees in large companies, newsletters are useful for sharing personal or unit achievements with coworkers and colleagues. They also provide opportunities for administrators to discuss issues affecting the entire work force. Examples of in-house employer newsletters are weekly "Faculty News" printed in most colleges and universities and daily "Bulletin Boards" distributed to employees or department heads of large companies where usually fifty or more people work.

Helpful Hints

Newsletters require a different writing style from publications of greater length. Remember that informational media sources are devoted to news items rather than lengthy detailed scientific treatises. The following practices can be useful if you are beginning your professional writing career.

1. Read several newsletters to develop a feel for the style of writing and topics presented. Develop an appreciation for what "makes" news. Select a newsletter or two to which you wish to submit a brief article.
2. Call the newsletter editor to learn more about the needs of the publication, such as:
    a. Does the newsletter have a staff of paid writers? Will it accept unsolicited articles?

     b. What is the recommended length of articles (i.e., number of words or pages)?

     c. Are there any topics or issues that the editor specifically would like to see addressed?

     d. What deadline dates must be observed for submitting articles? Remember, newsletters are published frequently, so a backlog of accepted material generally is waiting to be published.

     e. What is the acceptable format for submitted articles? Should they be double-spaced? Must they be printed in letter quality if a computer printer is used, or is draft mode acceptable?

     f. To whom should articles be submitted (e.g., directly to the editor, to the managing editor, to a copy editor)?

3. Never use pressure to try to get your article printed.
4. When writing your article, remember the following tips:

     a. Be able to support your remarks even when a newsletter does not include reference citations.

     b. Always be accurate. Your reliability and dependability as a news source determine your credibility.

     c. Place your conclusion first, then expand upon it. Remember, readers want to know what your news is within the first few sentences. If they find it interesting, they will continue reading.

     d. Use short sentences. Make your point and stop.

     e. Avoid jargon or acronyms. Use the language of the audience that reads the newsletter.

     f. Avoid posing hypothetical questions.

     g. Don't attack colleagues or employers individually if you disagree with their positions.

     h. Reread your article several times before sending it. Does it flow? Does it say what needs to be said at face value? Does a reader have to share your perspective to understand the gist of the article?

Although somewhat different in orientation than journals, we have found that newsletters offer the new academic an opportunity to get into print, to jump the first hurdle of professional publishing. With some practice the next step to more comprehensive and longer works becomes easier. For more experienced academics writing for newsletters helps bring well-roundedness to a career that promotion and tenure reviewers seek.

Getting to know newsletter editors is important. By taking time to call them, you are establishing personal contact, expressing an interest in their work, learning what they need in terms of content and style, and taking the first step toward establishing a publication record. The next chapter continues to stress the importance of developing rapport with editors by understanding the processes involved in writing for professional journals.

6

Creating Foothills From Mole Hills: Writing Journal Articles

Before submitting a manuscript to a journal for publication, it is wise to consider whether the selected journal is the right one for your paper. If the journal has an articulated scope or purpose, does your article match its interest? Is the journal's readership the audience you want to reach? What is the journal's general reputation? What is the lag time from receipt of your manuscript to its publication as an article? Does the journal use a peer-review process to judge submitted manuscripts? How frequently is the journal published? Who is the editor and to whom do you submit a manuscript?

The pressure to publish must be weighed carefully against the quality of the journal to which a paper is submitted (Fine 1987). Acceptance of a single paper by a well-reputed, widely circulated journal may be worth ten papers published in lesser known journals (Fine 1987). Your colleagues may be among the best judges of where your paper would be best published.

Whether and where a journal's articles are indexed is of particular salience to researchers. While a large circulation journal may assure immediate exposure of a research paper to a large audience, if that journal is not indexed, the article may be lost to future researchers because it is difficult (if not impossible) to retrieve through a literature search.

With these questions answered, you are better able to choose a journal for submission of your article. Once the journal is selected, however, a host of further questions are posed. Is your article written to the submission requirements of that particular journal? Is it too long, too brief? Can it be published as an article or as a letter? Does your style conform to the journal's style requirements?

The answers to many of these questions are often found in the journals themselves. Frequently, a review of past issues of a particular journal will be instructive in terms of what topics are of interest. The "Information for Authors" section, included in each issue of most major journals, provides detailed specifications regarding length, style, footnotes, and referencing citations. Often a statement regarding the scope or purpose of the journal is included in this section as well. Journal offices themselves also should be able to answer specific technical questions related to how the submission process works.

This chapter provides special help for writers seeking to publish in journals. Seven areas are discussed: (1) why journals operate, (2) the editorial process, (3) the review process, (4) manuscript development, (5) manuscript components, (6) the manuscript checklist, and (7) dealing with rejection.

Why Journals Operate

According to Glenn (1976), journals perform at least three major functions. The first of these is to "serve as vehicles for the dissemination of new knowledge" (Hood 1984, p. 17). Underlying this role is an understanding that publications are expected to influence and change the attitudes and behaviors of those who read them. Research, criticism, theories, and ideas of various kinds are likely to improve performance, aid in development of new technology, or speed innovations. Articles are simply a means by which professionals communicate their findings to others. More durable and tangible than radio and television interviews, and more comprehensive than conference and seminar presentations, journal articles are available for review as long as they are printed, collected, stored, and indexed.

The second function of journals is what has come to be known as the "gatekeeper" function (Glenn 1976). This function is performed principally by journal reviewers who determine whether manuscripts conform to style and formatting prerequisites as well as contribute to the body of knowledge characterized by the purpose of the journal and its occupational field.

The third function of scholarly periodicals is the personal recognition and rewards authors receive with publication. "Indeed . . . journals have become a part of the social process that constitutes a professional discipline" (Hood 1984, p. 17). With between 40,000 to 60,000 journals currently in circulation an author has a real opportunity to find an outlet in an appropriate source (Haney 1988). As noted in Chapter 2 (see Figure 2.2), the academic career path to status and visibility may be accomplished through writing and/or professional association activities. For many in academia, publications are the principal method used to disseminate and impart their messages.

The Editorial Process

The editorial process begins when an author submits a manuscript to a journal. Although each journal has its unique modifications to the editorial process, the vast majority follow very similar steps. Editors examine submissions to assure that they are complete and follow the guidelines of the journal. Some manuscripts are rejected at this point because of inadequate preparation or topical coverage outside the scope and purpose of the journal (Eichorn and VandenBos 1985). It should be noted as well that the guidelines of most scholarly journals, in keeping with the ethical standards and practices of most professional associations, do not condone simultaneous submission of a manuscript to multiple publishers (Hoover 1980).

Some contend, however, that submission to more than one journal at a time would result in better journals. The best work would "be snapped up by the most efficient, aggressive journals" (Leslie 1989, p. 127). Our experience has shown us that aggressiveness is not a commendable academic trait and that efficiency may be substituted by speed and lack of quality. The slow inefficient journals soon lack for articles and respect, and the effective quality journals abound not only in manuscripts but eminence. Journals that are slow and slovenly soon become known. Often such a shift from quality to mediocrity comes with a change of editorship.

Most journals require an original and a specified number of copies of each manuscript received. The original suggests that the manuscript has not been sent to other publications simultaneously, although computer printouts provide an opportunity for copies to be original in appearance. The original copy is assigned a manuscript number and kept on file by the editor. Copies are sent to reviewers for their comments and suggestions. Depending on the extensiveness of a journal's review process, the number of copies (specified in addition to the original draft) may vary from two to six. Editors appreciate authors who attach their title page to the original draft by paper clip rather than by stapling. Since your manuscript frequently may be reviewed without knowledge of its author, editors must remove evidence of your identity (i.e., letter of intent, title page, biographical sketch) before sending copies to reviewers. Paper clipped attachments make the editor's job a bit easier. Overall "a manuscript with a professional appearance obviously appeals to editors" (Noble 1989, p. 98).

After receiving your submission, editors acknowledge receipt by letter or postcard informing the principal author of the assigned manuscript number and an approximate date when the review will be completed. Many journals delegate initiation and monitoring of manuscript reviews to associate editors. Associate editors briefly scan manuscripts to determine which reviewers have an interest and acknowledged expertise in the topic submitted before sending copies to them. Depending on the publication, two to four reviewers are used for each manuscript. Sometimes a blend of editorial advisory board members and consulting or ad hoc reviewers are used.

After a manuscript has been reviewed, its status is reported by the associate editor to the editor who informs the author(s) of reviewer recommendations. Once a manuscript has been accepted for publication, the editor assembles accepted articles and decides the order in which they will be presented in an issue. Next, the editor (or managing editor) coordinates the layout of the issue with the printer.

Usually printers transfer manuscripts to an initial type setup called a galley. Galleys are returned to the journal editor who sends them to authors for proofreading. At this point, corrections beyond grammar and typographical errors should be minimal. Once galleys have been proofread and returned by authors to the editor, the printer makes the

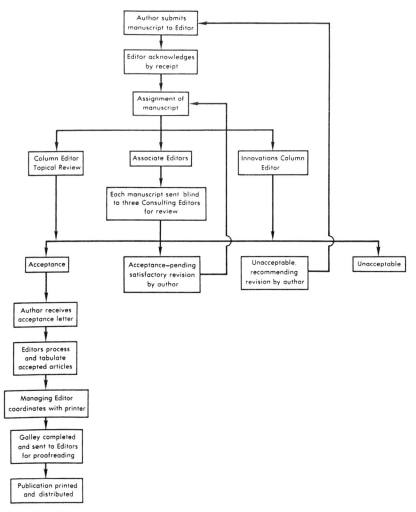

Figure 6.1a. The editorial process of journal articles. Adapted from T. F. Riggar and D. R. Maki. 1980. Stages of professional writing: A guide to authors. *Vocational Evaluation and Work Adjustment Bulletin* 13(1): 9–12. Reprinted with permission.

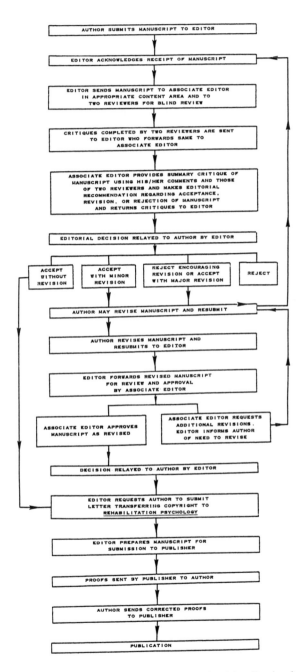

Figure 6.1b. The editorial process of journal articles. Reprinted with permission from *Rehabilitation Psychology*, a journal of the Division of Rehabilitation Psychology of the American Psychological Association.

noted corrections and begins final printing. Figure 6.1 provides a detailed flow chart of the typical editorial process from the time an author submits a manuscript to its completion as a printed article.

The Review Process

Journal reviewers are selected by editors and/or editorial advisory boards for recognized knowledge and expertise in specific areas of a profession. Most scholarly journals use what is called a blind, refereed process to assess the quality of a manuscript. "Blind" simply means that reviewers do not know the identity of writers and vice versa. "Refereed" means that more than one reviewer judges the suitability of manuscripts for publication in terms of writing style, topical area of interest, length and format, and other factors identified in the sample checklists of Figure 6.2.

Although some studies reveal insignificant differences between refereed and nonrefereed journals (Smith and Gough 1984), university deans and department chairs generally give more weight to publications in blind refereed journals when making promotion and tenure decisions (Suppa and Zirkel 1983). Yet, some controversy surrounds these matters. Surwillo (1986) and McGiffert (1988) suggest that perhaps reviews should not be performed blindly, recommending instead that the identities of reviewers and authors should be known to each other. Mirman (1975) feels that this "identity-known" method would be a possible incentive for reviewers to produce higher quality reviews in a timely manner. Regardless whether one supports blind or nonblind review, novice writers will learn that a major concern with manuscript submission is slow turnaround time among reviewers.

Depending on the journal, the size of its staff, number of reviewers available, and backlog of accepted articles awaiting publication, the review process generally takes two to six months to complete from date of submission to initial reviewer recommendations. Sometimes reviews may take as long as a year to complete, especially if the number of available reviewers is limited, the manuscript topic is sufficiently complex and/or has potential major significance to its field, or reviewers fail to inform editors of impending vacations, leaves of absence, or job changes. In one case, for example, a tentatively accepted manuscript needing revision was returned to its author with a note indicating a two-year publication backlog. The author was advised to consider the lag before resubmitting the paper for a second review. Walker (1987) found that for 43 percent of journals the time from acceptance to publication was twenty-six weeks or more. Henson (1988) determined for forty-nine education journals that an average publication decision (submission to accept/reject/revise) was eleven weeks with two to twenty-four months required for actual publication. Van Til (1986) reports that "on the average, a journal will publish an article about seven months after acceptance" (p. 253). Such a time delay obviously can be a source of anxiety for beginning writers. Indeed, Rodman (1970) reminds editors and referees of their ethical responsibility to perform their work promptly and without sacrificing quality. A time delay can be a source of anxiety for beginning writers to such a degree that Leslie (1990) found that "time required for an accepted article to be published" (p. 161) was the greatest source of dissatisfaction.

When a referee receives a manuscript for review, often it is accompanied by a standardized form for comments. Figure 6.2 provides examples used by journals when requesting evaluation, comments, and recommended disposition of papers. Many editors also ask reviewers to provide sufficient constructive comments to aid authors when making revisions. These comments may be in a separate section of the form, on a separate page, or written directly on the manuscript copy.

In conjunction with or in addition to specific questions asked of reviewers on the evaluation forms, certain manuscript components are ranked as more important than others. According to Frantz (1968), the most important criterion is the paper's potential contribution to the knowledge base of a field. This is followed by the "design of the study, objectivity in reporting results, topic selection, writing style and readability, and practical implications" (p. 385). Many journal editors examine submitted manuscripts and find common problems with "slight, trivial, or low quality work/research" which they note even before whether the manuscript is an "inappropriate subject for journal" (Noble 1989, p. 100). Added to this hierarchy, another study found that submissions which revealed statistical significance are three times

JOURNAL OF REHABILITATION
MANUSCRIPT REVIEWER'S GUIDELINES

The Journal of Rehabilitation is concerned with the publication of manuscripts that can improve the readership's understanding of various disabling conditions and assist in the advancement of professional practice across a broad range of rehabilitation disciplines. Since the Journal of Rehabilitation is intended for the total membership of the National Rehabilitation Association, the majority of manuscripts published in the Journal should have wide readership appeal. Likewise, the Journal is interested in the publication of manuscripts which report innovative practices, describe new rehabilitation principles and techniques, or discuss controversial and timely issues since such manuscripts can provide the basis for improved rehabilitation practice.

In addition to presenting relevant content, manuscripts selected for publication in the Journal of Rehabilitation should be well written, logically organized, easy to follow by a broad range of readers, and adhere to the reference style employed in previous issues of the Journal which closely follows practices suggested in the Publication Manual of the American Psychological Association. Of course, research-oriented manuscripts should clearly disclose the research problem, present a review of related literature, describe the methods and procedures employed, accurately analyze the data obtained, and discuss the findings in relation to the research problem.

With this in mind, please review the attached manuscript for possible publication in the Journal of Rehabilitation. Feel free to make whatever comments or editorial changes that you would like to make directly on the body of the manuscript or on a separate sheet of paper. Comments or editorial changes that might assist the author(s) in revising this manuscript or in preparing future manuscripts are especially helpful.

A clearly written review probably contains two elements. Grammatically, it is readable to both editor and author(s). Second, it is both concrete and specific enough that the author can make operational sense of what is being said, what the criticism is, what suggestions are being made, etc. Sweeping criticisms (such as, "this paper has little to offer") without specific examples of what is impeding the paper's contribution are unhelpful. It is helpful, however, to give specific illustrations of problems, suggestions, etc.

Authors need to receive clear feedback on which suggestions for revision should be required vs. which ones the reviewer simply thinks the author should consider. This applies regardless of whether or not the reviewer recommends acceptance. If the manuscript is rejected the author will still have a sense of the importance of each suggestion.

It is recognized that the length of a review is only one indicator of its thoroughness. At the same time, it might be helpful to reviewers to know my view of the minimum length of a sound (qua thorough) review. Experience suggests that it is most difficult to perform a thorough review in less than half a page (single-spaced, typed). On the other hand, reviews that are much more than two single-spaced pages may reflect over-editing.

When you have completed your review of this manuscript, please advise me regarding its acceptability for publication in the Journal of Rehabilitation by completing the form attached.

Figure 6.2a. Manuscript reviewer's guidelines. Reprinted with permission from the *Journal of Rehabilitation*, National Rehabilitation Association.

MANUSCRIPT EVALUATION FORM
JOURNAL OF REHABILITATION

Reviewer: _____ Date Sent:_____ Date Due:_____

Title of Manuscript: _____

Please read this manuscript with care using the rating criteria listed below. If the manuscript is outside your area of expertise or if you cannot review it by the above due date, please return it immediately.

MANUSCRIPT EVALUATION CRITERIA:

		NOT APPLICABLE	DEFINITELY NOT	NO	NEUTRAL	YES	DEFINITELY YES
1.	The topic is of current interest.	____	____	____	____	____	____
2.	The article is based on a sound rationale.	____	____	____	____	____	____
3.	The article was prepared according to APA style.	____	____	____	____	____	____
4.	The article accurately reviews relevant literature.	____	____	____	____	____	____
5.	The article is based on sound research design and data analysis.	____	____	____	____	____	____
6.	The author reaches reasonable conclusions based upon the data analysis.	____	____	____	____	____	____
7.	The article has practical implications for rehabilitation.	____	____	____	____	____	____
8.	The article stimulates further thought, study, or research.	____	____	____	____	____	____
9.	The article is readable and well-written.	____	____	____	____	____	____
10.	Abstract is clear, concise, and reflects article's content.	____	____	____	____	____	____

RECOMMENDATIONS:

I.   ACCEPT _____

    1. _____ No revisions.
    2. _____ Minor revisions as noted in comments.
    3. _____ Major revisions as noted in comments.

II. REJECT _____

    1. _____ Rework and resubmit.
    2. _____ Rework and submit to another Journal, e.g., _____
    3. _____ Article appears to be unpublishable even with major revisions.

COMMENTS:

    Record your comments in typewritten form on a separate sheet. Prepare them so that they may be directly conveyed to the author.

Figure 6.2b. Sample checklist used by journal reviewers. Reprinted with permission from the *Journal of Rehabilitation*, National Rehabilitation Association.

Association For Supervision And Curriculum Development
125 North West Street, Alexandria, VA 22314
(703) 549-9110 ext. 177
Manuscript Evaluation

EDUCATIONAL LEADERSHIP

Manuscript Title:

Instructions: Please use the following questions to guide your consideration of the manuscript. If the responses which are provided seem inappropriate, use your own words in the comments section.

1.   Accuracy, Validity of Contents
     To what extent is the manuscript accurate in its portrayal of schools, society, views of others, and findings of research?

     _____ Extremely accurate, authoritative

     _____ Generally accurate, acceptable

     _____ Inaccurate in several important respects

Comments:

2.   Significance of Treatment
     To what extent is the author's treatment of the topic fresh, insightful, and significant?

     _____ A major contribution to educational thought and practice

     _____ A sound treatment of the subject; worth publishing

     _____ An acceptable treatment, but not especially original or insightful

Comments:

3.   Publish
     In your opinion, what priority should be given to this manuscript in comparison with others we might publish?

     _____ High priority; publish

     _____ Other manuscripts should have higher priority

Comments:

4.   Changes
     If the manuscript is published, what changes are needed?

     _____ None, other than the usual minor editing

     _____ Needs the following changes

Comments:

Your name: _____

Telephone: _____ Date: _____

Figure 6.2c. Sample checklist used by journal reviewers. Reprinted with permission from *Educational Leadership*. Copyright 1987, the American Vocational Association.

General Guidelines for Reviewers

The Rehabilitation Counseling Bulletin publishes theoretical and research articles on rehabilitation-related topics. Traditionally, RCB has had the reputation of publishing only articles of the highest quality and of the greatest interest to the readership. All reviewers should adopt a critical, but constructive mind set in reviewing articles. There is no room for either over-critical persecution or unconditional positive regard for submitted papers. In almost every case, reviewers will find it possible to make suggestions that will improve the article. If an article is marginal, a conservative stance is suggested, i.e., recommend the paper be rejected, but reworked and resubmitted. This tact puts the Editors in a stronger position to encourage authors to modify the manuscripts or to reject the manuscript if there are several backlogged articles of similar content.

When reviewing an article, ask yourself the following specific questions:

1. Is the topic of the manuscript appropriate for RCB?

2. Was the article prepared according to APA style? Make sure to check the reference list to see if it follows APA style.

3. Is the length appropriate? Regular articles rarely exceed 15 manuscript pages. If a good article is longer, suggest ways the length may be reduced.

4. Frequently all tabular data can be adequately described in the text. Tables are expensive to print and take up space. Therefore the general editorial policy has been to print no tables when the data can reasonably be presented in the text.

5. For articles that may be of limited interest or for short manuscripts, the "In Brief" section may be most appropriate. Papers for "In Brief" should be 4 manuscript pages of text in addition to references, etc.

When you have finished reading the manuscript, please:

1. Fill out the Manuscript Review Form and return two copies.

2. Prepare and return two copies of your "Comments", which state your reactions and suggestions for revision. The Comments will be xeroxed and sent to the author. Usually one to two pages of comments are sufficient and should not state your recommendation regarding disposition.

3. You may retain the manuscript, but please return a copy if you have made substantive editorial comments in the body of the paper. If you retain the manuscript, and want to use it in your publication endeavors, you are ethically and legally bound to obtain the RCB Editor's and the author's permission for use. The Editor can supply the author's name.

Figure 6.2d. General guidelines for reviewers. Reprinted with permission from the *Rehabilitation Counseling Bulletin,* a journal of the American Rehabilitation Counseling Association.

more likely to be accepted than studies containing nonsignificant or only approaching significant results (Atkinson, Furlong, and Wampold 1982).

The purpose of the forms in Figure 6.2, and the review process itself, however, are not simply to accept or reject manuscripts. In most cases when manuscripts are unacceptable as submitted, editors offer suggestions to authors about ways to upgrade the manuscript to publishable quality and send reviewers' forms to provide further assistance. This degree of feedback provides emerging writers with an opportunity to learn from recognized experts and authorities in their field (Riggar and Maki 1980).

Authors whose manuscripts are not accepted after the first review have to make a decision: revise the manuscript and resubmit it to the same journal, submit the draft to another journal, or quit. Forman (1988) notes that there is "usually a point when the writer wishes to scuttle the project. . . . Fortunately, this (fantasizing abandonment) phase usually ends" (p. 182). Although far too many choose the last option, "continued efforts at writing and submitting (and learning from the unsuccessful attempts) will result in eventual publishing success" (Eichorn and VandenBos 1985, p. 1315).

Manuscript Development

Most manuscripts begin as an idea derived from self-experience, reading, and/or listening. Writers then begin a process of integrating their ideas with the substance of their professions into themes and topics. Emotion often leads the way toward generating manuscripts based on interest, attitudes, and reactions writers feel for topics about which they care enough to invest the time and effort needed to write about them. As more personal energy and time are invested in the project, however, emotionally laden content is replaced gradually with increasingly objective presentation.

After developing an idea, the next step in the process generally involves reviewing the available literature about the topic. Reading and researching provide additional sources of information and views of others who previously have examined the same or similar topics.

Keeping detailed and copious notes about each citation initially builds a set of references that are used when writing the first manuscript draft.

If not performed prior to reviewing the literature, the next step is to develop an outline of the manuscript. If an outline was developed to sketch the original idea first, now is an excellent time to revise it in conjunction with information acquired from the literature review. Developing an outline provides a schematic guide for the paper, as well as a topical focus to enhance motivation. In other words, writing seems to be much less tedious and overwhelming when it is performed in manageable segments characterized by the elements making up the outline.

After developing an outline, some experts suggest sending query letters to editors to assess their interest in the proposed manuscript (Dorn 1985a). Other experts, however, note that many editors neither encourage nor desire query letters (Henson 1984, 1988). Perhaps the most appropriate suggestion is to call an editor first to learn his or her preference.

Although the actual writing process itself is highly individualized, there are certain constant factors evident in the literature and from experience. First, know your intended audience. "Typically, the manuscript will initially be submitted to a journal that is well known and read regularly by the contributor" (Rodman 1978, p. 235). By reading numerous articles published in the journal to which a manuscript will be sent, writers should notice a general writing style that distinguishes the printed contributions. This journal style, however, should not be confused with an individual's writing style (word usage, phrasing, etc.). Instead, journal style refers to a general content and/or topical theme which seems to permeate issues and possibly distinguishes a journal from others.

Individual writing style develops with time and practice. There are several tips, however, that may be beneficial. Woodring (1981) advises writers to begin with "a strong opening . . . [and] strive for brevity. Select strong [action] verbs and exactly the right nouns . . . avoid the use of vogue words, euphemisms and jargon" (p. 500). Flory (1983) strongly urges writers to avoid cluttering manuscripts with inappropriate, long, complex, and seldom used words. Furthermore, Dillon (1981) cautions authors against using writing tricks known as "titular

1. Start with an idea.

2. Develop a rough outline of the topic and its coverage.

3. Review available topical literature.

4. Take copious notes from relevant literature.

5. Evaluate and revise the initial outline.

6. Contact the journal editor about interest in your topic.

7. Begin writing a rough draft of the manuscript.

8. Examine the journal style of the selected periodical.

9. Examine the draft for "absolute" terms—modify as needed.

10. Review and rewrite (polish) the manuscript draft.

11. Examine the manuscript for mistakes (e.g., typos).

12. Ask for suggestions from others as needed.

13. Review all suggestions that were solicited.

14. Incorporate suggestions as appropriate.

15. Reexamine the "final" initial draft before sending.

Figure 6.3. Elements of manuscript development.

colonicity." This refers to a predominant characteristic of scholarly publications wherein nearly 72 percent of article titles are extensive, dysrhythmic, and overuse colons. Take the title of this chapter, for example: "Creating Foothills From Mole Hills: Writing Journal Articles." Certainly there are other titles that are as informative without using a colon. Interestingly enough, the degree to which titles are important is of sufficient merit for books to have been written on the topic (Bodian 1988).

Hoover (1980) reiterates Sikula's caution (see Chapter 4) about using absolute statements characterized by words such as "always," "never," "good," "bad," "right," and "wrong." Use qualified statements instead which are potentially less offensive to readers, characterized by words such as "apparently," "tend," "sometimes," "may," and "occasionally." These points are especially important in an academic environment where writing is a "way of joining and continuing a tradition . . . to say something and to say it well" (Wolper 1982, p. 155). Writing is a way of giving back to the field and to colleagues some of what has been given the author through literature reviews and the learning process.

Once completed, a drafted manuscript needs to be thoroughly reviewed, rewritten if necessary, and examined for mistakes. When a collaborative writing project is involved, each author should review the draft independently at first followed by mutual consultation seeking final agreement. Additional preliminary reviews may be obtained from friends, spouses, and advisory groups when feasible (Ostrowski and Bartel 1985; Sikula 1979).

Manuscript Components

Manuscript materials mailed to an editor include more than just a text. They consist of a letter of intent and multiple copies of a title page, the manuscript body, references, and, perhaps, an author biographical sketch. For many manuscripts, additional details may be required. These include such things as the style of typing and presentation used, camera- or printer-ready figures, tables, illustrations, and pictures, and permission to reprint. Later in the process, galley or page proofs may be sent through the mail.

Letter of Intent

The cover letter from the author should state the title of the manuscript and a request to have the paper reviewed for possible publication. In some cases authors should indicate whether the submission is a general feature article or one intended for a specific column or section of the publication (e.g., theory, research, practice).

Title Page

After the letter of intent, a title page must accompany the original manuscript draft. In addition to the proposed title of the article, the title page should include the author's name and employment affiliation.

References

No matter how often writers check their references, it is not unusual for some to appear in the reference list but not in the body of the manuscript or vice versa. Sometimes this oversight results from numerous rewrites when citations are moved, removed, or added. Sometimes spelling errors in authors' names occur or publication dates are mistyped. In any event, nothing reveals sloppy scholarship to an editor and reviewers more than references gone astray. Similarly, be certain to adhere rigorously to the journal's most current adopted style of citing references (e.g., Smith, A. B., R. P. Jones, and P. M. Collins. 1987. Cognitive restructuring during a bear market. *Journal of Business Psychology* 24(2):123–27.).

Biographical Sketch

Some journals request a biographical sketch. The information provided by authors may be as brief as the person's name, current job title, and place of employment, or more lengthy to include academic degrees and where they were conferred, pertinent work experiences, organizational memberships and offices held, significant publications and awards, and general interest in the field. Vitae or resumes are not brief biographical sketches and should not be sent in lieu of the above.

Typing and Presentation

Although it may seem trite, book editors seem to enjoy seeing, reading, and touching manuscripts with crisp and clear words printed or typed on bonded or at least 25 percent cotton rag paper. Although journal editors do not seem to share the same penchant, writers should be aware that manuscript appearance conveys a sense of professionalism. Be certain that the typewriter or printer has a relatively new ribbon. Using a new ribbon in a conventional typewriter for the first time, however, may increase the likelihood of smudging. For those with dot-matrix printers especially, a new ribbon tends to saturate the paper with ink. Type on only one side of a page, never on both sides unless specifically requested by the journal's guidelines. Be especially mindful of typing within the page margins recommended by the journal. Neither accept nor send copies that are too light, too dark, or misaligned.

Another comment must be made about using computer printers. There are basically three types: impact, dot-matrix, and laser printers. Impact printers use an interchangeable "daisy wheel" containing characters of a specific font style (for example, pica, elite, gothic, or script). Different fonts are selected by changing the daisy wheel. Impact printers transfer characters to paper much like a conventional typewriter. Dot-matrix printers, on the other hand, form characters through a series of pins that can be programmed to a variety of fonts. They are very popular because of their font versatility and higher printing speed. When selecting a dot-matrix printer, however, look for one with at least "near letter-quality" capability. For example, a 9-pin head is capable of "draft" and near letter quality, but usually not letter quality, this requiring a 24-pin head. Also, the fewer the number of pins used, the faster the printing speed but at the sacrifice of character quality. Laser printers are the most expensive. They produce exceptionally crisp and clean letter quality at a speed somewhere between impact and dot-matrix printers.

Figures, Tables, Illustrations, and Pictures

Editors generally prefer to minimize the number of figures, tables, illustrations, and pictures in a manuscript. Each are more expensive to reproduce than narrative text, and they sacrifice space that could be used for other articles, announcements, or advertising. A blank page costs nearly as much as one filled with information because journals usually purchase a fixed number of pages, known as signatures, from their printers. When figures and the like are indispensable, be certain they conform to the following standards whenever possible:

1. Prepare printer-ready tables, figures, and illustrations. For black line art, such as figures, tables, and some illustrations, this is accomplished by having a PMT (photomechanical transfer) made of each. For other figures or illustrations consisting of multiple colors or shades of

1. Letter of intent to the journal editor (includes article title, request for review, and general area where it may fit into the journal). Attach with a paper clip.

2. Title page (includes the article title, author's name, and employment affiliation). Attach with a paper clip.

3. Biographical sketch (includes a brief statement identifying the author, current employment and job title, and possibly major professional awards, offices, and/or contributions to the field). Optional. Attach with a paper clip.

4. Abstract or executive summary (summarizes the article in 100 words or less).

5. Article narrative (begins with the title of the manuscript followed by the information to be communicated — see Table 1.1 in Chapter 1).

6. References (includes only those citations used in the manuscript as compared to a bibliography that includes other relevant sources although not necessarily cited in the article).

7. Tables, figures, illustrations, pictures (includes original forms used in the article, but not necessarily the original printer-ready proofs or negatives).

8. Permission to reprint (includes all signed documents giving the author permission to include previously published materials).

Figure 6.4. Manuscript components.

grey, a black-and-white photograph should be taken of each and printed preferably on glossy paper.

2. Submit only copies of the original tables, figures, and illustrations at first submission. Save the photographs and PMTs until the manuscript has been accepted for publication unless otherwise indicated by the editor.

3. When an article has been accepted for publication, send both the PMTs and photographs. The printer may wish to reduce their size further, or compare the readability of both after galleys are printed.

4. Never discard or send (unless specifically requested by the journal) the negatives of printer-ready materials.

Permission to Reprint

Whenever a table, figure, illustration, picture, or quotation is taken from another source permission to reprint is required for its use. This rule applies even to your own manuscripts that have appeared as articles because the "source" is now the journal. Most often journals will provide permission if requested in writing. Be certain to clearly specify the original source (volume, issue, and title), the intended purpose for the request (how the materials will be used), and leave a space for the releasing authority to sign and date your request (acknowledging and/or giving permission for copying). On occasion, editors or publishers require a nominal fee, a similar release from the author of the original work, or a copy of the completed manuscript when published that uses the material. (Note that any fees required will not be paid unless the article is accepted for publication.) Finally, be absolutely certain to include a copy of the signed release permission (not the original unless specified by the editor) with your letter of intent and manuscript.

Galleys and Page Proofs

Galleys represent the printer's initial typesetting of a manuscript — before being made into pages — often without tables or other similar nontext content included. A set of page proofs, on the other hand, is the entire manuscript (including nontextual matter) as it will appear in the journal. Page proofs show the division of the material in final page lengths. Whether an author receives galleys or page proofs depends on the policies and procedures of the journal and/or publisher. In either instance, however, galleys and proofs represent the last opportunity for authors to make minor corrections (e.g., typographical errors). Many editors require authors to sign the proofs as evidence of final approval before they go to press.

Manuscript Checklist

Performing the activities covered in this book to this point will not ensure manuscript publication when a paper has little to say or is written poorly. Although the review forms in Figure 6.2 provide insight into the crucial elements that are evaluated in a manuscript, more

1. Completeness

_____ goals and objectives are clearly stated

_____ purpose of the article is achieved

_____ ramifications are identified

_____ solutions are presented

_____ presentation of material is fully logical and coherent

_____ unnecessary information has been removed

_____ information is succinct yet comprehensive

_____ significance of the information is apparent

2. Authoritativeness

_____ references are relevant to the topic

_____ proportional mixture of author and others' works

_____ all relevant major sources are cited

_____ occupational disciplinary blinders are removed

_____ authorities from other fields are cited

_____ information is up to date

_____ sources of assistance are acknowledged

_____ permissions to use others' work are obtained

3. Expertness

_____ proper methodology is used

_____ methodology has been applied appropriately

_____ novel or new methodology is justified

_____ reasons for using previously unused methods are sound

_____ methods are presented clearly

_____ methods can be replicated as identified

_____ purpose is to present method or findings

4. Singularity

_____ provides new information or confirms existing knowledge

_____ unique, original, or new elements are clearly revealed

_____ how old information may be used by others is stated

_____ applicability to salient groups is identified

_____ information that is presented is timely

_____ information is specialized or generalizable

_____ those who could use the information are identified

_____ reasons for using the information are identified

_____ the article improves the existing body of knowledge

5. Quality

_____ article follows journal guidelines

_____ correct grammar, syntax, spelling, and punctuation used

_____ nonsexist language is used

_____ ethnic bias is absent

_____ "handicapping" language is absent (e.g., the disabled)

_____ information is presented in an orderly manner

_____ jargon and esoteric terms are absent

_____ communication is parsimonious

_____ article has been proofread

_____ original and copies have a clean appearance

Table 6.1. Manuscript checklist.

information is needed for novice writers. Perhaps the most thorough manuscript checklist available for academic authors is provided by Reitt (1984). Because of its extensiveness, however, a modified version appears below:

1. *Completeness of the article as written:* What issue does your article attempt to present and/or solve? Does it achieve its purpose? What ramifications are possible based on the presented solution? Is the significance of the issue and solution apparent to the reader?

2. *Authoritativeness of the article:* What are the sources of information used by the article? Is the information based excessively on

either the author's work or that of others? Does the presentation suggest that the author is ignorant of relevant sources from other occupational disciplines? Have important authorities on the subject (both within and external to the author's field) been ignored? Do quotations and references carry the article instead of the author's writing? Have acknowledgments been made and releases been obtained?

3. *Expertness of the article:* Has the proper methodology been used upon which to base the conclusions of the article? Has the method been used correctly? Is the method new or a novel approach to a traditional design? Is the method a resurrection of a previously unused, abandoned, or borrowed design? If it is, how is its use justified? Is the purpose of the article to present a new, novel, or resurrected method, and/or solution to a problem? Has the method been described clearly and sufficiently for purposes of replication by readers?

4. *Singularity of the article:* Does the article provide new information or confirm an existing body of knowledge? If the information is not new, how is it different or in what manner has it been overlooked by others before? Is the information timely? Who needs to know the information presented, and why?

5. *Quality of the article:* Is the finished article fully refined? Are there typographical errors? Is correct punctuation used? Are sentences and/or paragraphs too long? Are sentences and paragraphs connected by transitions? Does the article use correct grammar and syntax?

Dealing With Rejection

Throughout this book the recurring message is that academic writing requires patience, practice, and perseverance. Eichorn and VandenBos (1985) speculate that "the vast majority of authors with 40 to 50 journal publications have had that many (and generally more) rejections" (p. 1315). Indeed, these authors found an initial rejection rate of 98 percent. Acceptance of revised manuscripts, though, is between 20 and 40 percent, resulting in a corrected rejection rate of approximately 75 percent. This matches an examination by Henson (1988) who found an average rejection rate of 72 percent by the forty-nine education journals in his survey. Although most efforts eventually become published when authors persist, as demonstrated by Tryon and Kokaska (see Chapter 4), some manuscripts are simply filed away.

Many years ago we both worked on an article that we submitted to an important journal in our field. The manuscript was rejected some three months later. The article was not rejected suggesting revision or advice, simply rejected overall. We examined the seventeen points of criticism and did a minor rewrite of three points. We then sent the manuscript to a respected international journal where it was "Accepted as is" and published some six months later. It did not take us long upon examining the original return manuscript to determine that only one reviewer had examined the document. The editor then had apparently read the review and reiterated the comments. We knew this to be the case as the second set of return comments were too similar to the first review (many items of which were simply nonsense) and because one of us happened to have a copy of the editor's handwriting on an acceptance from a year before. We learned then that not all criticism is done well and not all journals or at least all editors follow the prescribed process all the time. For several years the published article had quite a number of reprint requests.

Conversely we once did a rather lengthy research study during which we had promised about twelve people copies of the final product for their assistance with the research. We decided to write a sort of minimonograph first to send to those who had helped and then to produce a journal manuscript for submission. The final product was about three times normal journal manuscript size and packed with figures and tables. After favorable feedback we decided to simply send it in as a regular article submission and let the editor and editorial advisory board tell us what to cut. A few months later we were notified that the "journal manuscript" was "Accepted pending minor revision." The revision entailed the elimination of two figures and adding to several parts of the minimonograph/journal manuscript.

Writers should not be discouraged by criticism and rejection, although such advice is easier given than taken. In many cases, editors include reviewer comments, suggestions, additional suggested references, and the like to authors when the review process has been completed. These notes constitute means through which authors can learn how to improve their writing to satisfy their colleagues and their profession. Even accomplished authors who have mastered the mechanics of writing and publishing learn with every project. Reviewer feedback and criticism are vital to the overall publishing process. Needless to say, it is far more comforting to receive anonymous criticism early than to read or hear about it in print associated with your name (e.g., letters to the editor).

Markland (1983) cites two basic principles of seeking and using criticism. Seek critical evaluation only if you really want it, and refrain from attempting to disprove your critic's evaluation. Markland suggests that there are eight constructive comments made so frequently that indeed they may constitute a guide for critics. These words probably will be written on or about your rejected manuscript. Remember, they are about your manuscript, not you.

1. Not appropriate. Your manuscript is too specialized, too general, or for a different journal or different audience.
2. Homework not done. Expert reviewers know when you have missed something essential.
3. Introductory. Your manuscript sounds or reads like a class presentation.
4. Nothing new. Your manuscript is old hat to the reviewers.
5. Wrong, inaccurate. Check your references again.
6. Not clear. Try a different approach.
7. Detail. Your manuscript has too much or too little detail.
8. Badly written. Though this is just opinion, referees are experienced authors (pp. 144–45).

Barriers to publication can be reduced by following the systematic and practiced methods of developing manuscripts as advocated by professional journals. Mastering mechanics will not ensure publication unless writers have developed the ability to communicate something worthwhile clearly.

7

Expanding the Horizons:
Monographs and Technical Reports

Thousands of technical reports and monographs are published annually in this country alone. In spite of this wide variety, most monographs and technical reports share several things in common. Most are the end product of studies and investigations typically funded by public or private nonprofit agencies. Nearly all provide detailed and specific accounting of background issues, procedures and methodologies used, outcomes and discussions, limitations that can affect generalized use of reported results, and implications for future research, policy decisions, training, or remedial activities.

This chapter describes a general model for technical reports and monographs. Because of their similarity to articles (Chapter 6) and books (Chapter 8), we have limited our discussion to: (1) the characteristics of monographs and technical reports, (2) front matter, (3) narrative body, and (4) concluding sections. The objective of the chapter is to familiarize readers with the nature and scope of these written materials. Reports such as these are often required by local, state, regional, and national fund-granting agencies.

Distinguishing Characteristics

Two characteristics immediately come to mind that distinguish monographs and technical reports from scholarly articles and books. First, monographs and technical reports generally are much longer than articles and often shorter than books. Second, monographs generally are much more specific and detailed in their focus than either articles or books. Monographs and technical reports typically are written about a specific project, for a very limited audience. Other less obvious characteristics also differentiate these reports, such as length, appearance, binding, publishing sources, and contracts.

Length and Appearance

Monographs (which will include technical reports hereafter) range from about 40 to 150 or 200 pages, averaging approximately 60 to 80 pages. These reports typically use single-spaced typing instead of the double-spaced formats required by book and journal publishers. In some cases, such as reports for federal agencies, pages may be typed on both sides of the page as well. Finally, tables and figures usually are incorporated within the body of the report instead of attached to the end of chapters or at the end of the entire manuscript.

Binding and Publishing

Monographs frequently are bound in soft covers rather than in hard covers. Soft binding can be accomplished by simply gluing pages on the spine side to the cover, gluing and stapling, drilling a series of holes to accommodate a flexible plastic binding spine, or riveting a more rigid plastic spine.

Monographs used as training manuals, or intended to be updated periodically, generally have two or three drilled holes for use with a ringed binder. Regardless of the method selected, they seldom use the more expensive procedures of gluing, stitching, and hard-cover attachment typically reserved for books and reference works.

Unless a monograph is produced totally by its authors, publishers usually perform binding activities along with printing and graphic layout. In order to keep costs to a minimum, especially when a limited number of copies are anticipated, publishers frequently use photocopied reproductions rather than more expensive typesetting methods. With the advent of microcomputing, word processing, desktop specialty graphics programs, plotters, and laser printers, however, monographs can closely approximate the appearance of more expensively produced publications at a fraction of the cost.

Contracts and Audiences

Most monographs represent the final product of funded grant proposals. Without question, the vast majority of grant findings are disseminated through monographs from governmental sources or private nonprofit foundations and agencies. Funded proposals generally include budget requests to pay for anticipated costs of printing and other publishing activities. Sometimes grants stipulate that the funding source owns all copyrights to reports and other materials emanating from the project. Sometimes these rights are negotiated after completion of the project among the funding source, the principal investigator, and the institution employing the investigator. Seldom are contracts between publishers and monograph authors part of the process as they are with books (see Chapter 8 about book contracts). Once a funding source has relinquished or waived its rights to ownership, however, authors may wish to enter into contracts with publishing houses in the event subsequent large-scale publishing and distribution are warranted.

As mentioned earlier, monographs address highly technical information about very specific topics (for example, a study to determine the need for and optimum procedures required to propagate earthworms in the Pacific Rim region). It is safe to assume, however, that interest in such specificity is limited to a handful of readers. Yet, monographs that can be used as training manuals, providing easy-to-follow "how-to" information for potential consumers, may indeed be reprinted in substantial numbers. Although monographs with this degree of popularity are rare (perhaps the notable exception being the President's Annual Executive Budget published each January), authors should be prepared to adjust their publication methods accordingly.

Front Matter

Among the elements of monographs presented in Chapter 1 were a number of initial components called the front matter. Many monographs begin with a brief summary of significant findings printed on the inside of the front cover. Often this brief account lists the important results of the project in easy-to-understand language without using numerical data except to draw attention (e.g., percentages). Following

A SYSTEMATIC ANALYSIS FOR EVALUATING
FISCAL MANAGEMENT OF UNIVERSITY RESOURCES

FINAL REPORT

Josephine L. Resnik, Director
John Q. Frankl, Research Associate

Fiscal Management Control Project
University of the Central Red Plains
Office of the Chancellor
3215 Youngstown Circle
Edwardsville, New York
10398

202/555-4321

April 1988

(Covers research performed from May 1, 1986, to March 30, 1988)

This study was supported in part by Research and Demonstration Grant GP01230001 from the National Institute of Educational and Fiscal Science, Office of Educational Administration, Kalamazoo, Michigan 48901

Figure 7.1. Example of a monograph title page.

this skeletal overview are the following components designated with Roman numeral pagination: title page, foreword, preface, table of contents, list of tables and figures, contributing and other significant advisory committees, and an abstract.

Title Page

This page identifies the title of the monograph as well as information including the project's director, location, date of report, inclusive periods covered by the monograph, and sources responsible for funding the project. Figure 7.1 is an example of a typical title page.

Foreword

The foreword generally is written by a person or persons with a vested interest in the report, such as a representative of the funding source or the director of the project. The foreword sets the stage and tone of the report and its perceived importance for those who will or may wish to use it.

Preface

The preface is written most often by the project director or in some cases the principal investigator. The preface offers a broad overview of the need for the information contained in the report, its purpose, and its perceived usefulness. It also recognizes specific individuals for their special contributions to the monograph.

Table of Contents

The table of contents lists all major sections and subsections of the monograph, ending with appendices. When appendices are not part of the report, the last entry is the reference section. Page numbers are given for each section and subsection. Lowercase Roman numerals are used to designate all sections before the introduction, and Arabic numbers are used thereafter.

List of Tables and Figures

Immediately following the table of contents is a list of tables and figures. Although some monographs list figures before tables, others use the reverse format. In either case, the typical entry follows a general format such as:

1. Table 1: General Description of Catchment Districts   30
2. Table 2: Average Time Utilization of Personnel   34
1. Figure 1: Ratio of Time and Cost for Services   15
2. Figure 2: Average Time Taken for Lunch by   22
   Department

Regardless of the order of presentation, it is important to list tables and figures separately instead of commingling them in the order they appear in the report.

Committees

One or more subsections may make up this component of the front matter. Lists of members' names and their respective project titles could include those who served on the steering committee, project staff, research design committee, project consultants, state project managers, regional project managers, national project managers, and external review team, among others.

Abstract

The abstract is a brief summary of the nature, scope, and important findings of the project. If space permits, a brief sentence or two identifying the procedures and any key words may be included. The abstract usually is confined to no more than 500 words (abbreviations generally count as one word, while hyphenated words sometimes count as two words). The abstract often makes up the last page(s) and is designated with Roman numerals.

Narrative Body

Arabic page numbers begin with the narrative portion and continue to the end of the manuscript. The narrative generally is composed of: (1) an overview of the project, (2) a literature review, (3) project activities, (4) results and discussion, (5) conclusions and recommendations, and (6) dissemination and utilization.

Overview of the Project

Among the subsections contained in the overview are: (1) introduction — usually no more than two paragraphs identifying salient reasons for undertaking the project; and (2) statement of the problem — a review of the critical problems that the project attempts to address and possibly remediate.

Literature Review

This section may stand alone or, in some cases, may be incorporated as part of the overview. When it is presented as a separate section, it often contains an extensive and sometimes exhaustive review and critique of all previous significant studies, research, and other efforts to resolve the problems addressed by the current project. Specific subsections in the literature review depend to a great extent on the topical area(s) of the subject of the project.

Project Activities

This section resembles the methodology portion in most journal articles. Among the variety of subsections contained in this section are: (1) participants — the people, groups, and agencies that were queried; (2) sampling methods — description of the techniques used to select participants to represent the population of which they are a part; (3) instrumentation — identification of devices used to collect information; (4) analyses — identification and justification of the methods used to analyze responses, behaviors, or outcomes of participants; (5) procedures — a thorough description of the nature, scope, sequence, time frames, and so forth of all activities; and (6) problems encountered — identification of procedural changes resulting from unforeseen events that altered the intended methods.

Results and Discussion

This section reports outcomes achieved by the project. Authors can assist readers by using subsection labels corresponding to those used in the project activities section. It is also common for authors to discuss findings within each subsection (rather than separately) in order to maintain continuity. Results are discussed in relation to findings of previous studies and similar projects. Summary tables and figures often are used to enhance comprehension.

Conclusions and Recommendations

This section provides further information about the overall meaning of the results. It also includes a subsection identifying important limitations of the project that could affect reliable interpretation, replication, and generalization of the findings reported. Based upon the results and noted limitations, a recommendations subsection concludes the section.

Dissemination and Utilization

The narrative body concludes with a detailed proposal concerning methods for communicating, using, and implementing the findings of the project. This section frequently sows the seeds for new projects or continuation of the current one for an extended period.

Concluding Sections

References

Immediately following the dissemination and utilization subsection is a complete listing of references cited in the narrative portion of the manuscript. The reference section is limited to those works actually appearing in the report. When a listing includes not only the cited references but also other related materials, the section is more appropriately called a bibliography.

Appendices

The last section of a monograph is reserved for more technical information such as complex statistical tables and analyses, instruments used for gathering information, instructions and other explanatory materials provided to participants, and proceedings of technical meetings. Materials developed from the findings of the project, such as training modules, lesson plans, and other similar products, are usually bound separately.

On the one hand, monographs resemble articles (or perhaps more properly, doctoral dissertations) with regard to their focus on a particular topic and its related problems. On the other hand, they resemble books in terms of length. In the next chapter about book publishing readers will quickly appreciate those significant differences between the respective contents of books and monographs.

8

Scaling the Summits: Your First Book

In 1978 approximately 40,000 books were published in the United States alone (Nelson 1978). By 1986 the total exceeded 52,000 (Grannis 1988), and the number continues to grow. The publication of a book is the pinnacle of the publishing pyramid; it represents the highest career attainment for most academicians. As Figure 1.2 in Chapter 1 revealed, there are many types of books corresponding to a variety of publishing outlets. With reasonable effort and persistence, most authors are capable of writing a book-length manuscript. Although many indeed do, only a fraction achieve publication. For example, Robinson and Higbee (1978) note that only 5 percent of book proposals receive contract offers from publishers, and less than half of university faculty ever have published a book (ACLS 1989; Bayer and Dutton 1977; Voeks 1962).

The purpose of this chapter is to tell potential authors what they need to know about the book-publishing process. It includes discussions of the publishing industry in general and book publishing in particular, how to prepare proposals and negotiate contracts, and, finally, how to work with editors.

Book Publishing

New academicians find that considerable differences exist between themselves and more experienced, established, and higher ranked faculty members regarding book publication. For example, McKeon (1983) suggests that writing a book involves more than the act of writing. It embodies knowing what to do the first time without unnecessary trial-and-error delays. This knowledge comes from an experience that generally new faculty simply have not had. Roskies (1975) indicates that other advantages of senior faculty often include a "waiting publisher, a competent secretarial staff, and an adequate . . . budget" (p. 1165). Although a publishing record may not assure that any author's current book proposal will be accepted by a publisher, a history of published manuscripts, and the status and professional visibility it gives, paves the way for acquiring resources (see Figure 2.2 in Chapter 2).

A publishing record enhances one's chances for acquiring organizational resources, support, and subsidies. Germano (1983) reports, for example, "the chances of securing a publication subsidy are almost two out of three at a private institution and almost 50/50 at a state institution" (p. 13). In addition to fiscal disbursement, some scholarly writers have "succeeded in being excused from the duller academic chores" (Roskies, 1975, p. 1165), been provided word processors for their offices (Hanna 1983), or been given other similar benefits.

Acquiring additional resources toward publication may enhance an author's potential productivity and efficiency. Perks alone, however, do not ensure increased ability to secure a publishing contract. To do this, an author must continue to demonstrate both effective scholarly and technical knowledge. Scholarly knowledge relies on acquired and demonstrated expertise of one's academic specialty. Technical knowledge about publishing, though, transcends occupations and is characterized by knowing who might publish your book. To discover this, a working knowledge is needed of the different types of publishers, their operations, and why they exist.

Writing a book is not unlike publishing an article in a professional journal. Both involve starting with an idea, performing research, writing, deciding where to submit the manuscript, rewriting, proofreading galleys, and receiving complimentary copies of the printed results. The difference between articles and books is merely a matter of degree of coverage. What constitutes the degree of difference can be explained best to potential book authors by "an editor who has the

Books Published		Publishers Assistance	
39%	1 book	16%	great help
38	2–3 books	43	some help
18	4–9 books	41	little or no assistance
5	10+ books	49%	help useful
		9	would have liked more assistance
Submitting the Manuscript			
8%	invited by publisher	3	wanted less publisher involvement
54	1 publisher		
16	2–5 publishers		
9	8+ publishers	**Production Time**	
3	10 publishers	90%	within 1 year
Presenting the Manuscript		**Royalties/Other compensation**	
82%	detailed outline	Hardcover	
72	cover letter	47%	10–15% royalties
57	1 or more chapters	Softcover	
51	provided their resumes	32%	10% royalties
Publishers' Marketing		Checks	
27%	excellent job	38%	annual royalty check
35	satisfied	50%+	twice annually
35	poor job	Free Copies	
1	no publicity	1–40 range; 10 most frequent	
Sales		Earnings	
Softcover		13%	less than $1,000
47%	less than 1,500	56	$1,000–$4,000
37	2,000–5,000	15	$5,000–$7,000
12	6,000–15,000	17	$10,000+
3	15,000+		
Hardcover		**Experience with Writing and Publishing**	
17%	less than 1,000	50%	very pleased
23	1,000–3,000	47	satisfied
25	4,000–8,000	0	disappointed
5	20,000+		
Writing Time			
9%	6 months		
43	1 year +		
36	1–2 years		
1	20 years		

Table 8.1. Outcome activities of publishing textbooks. Adapted from L. Seligman and S. C. Kelly. 1990. Writing and publishing books in counseling: A survey of authors. *Journal of Counseling and Development* 69(1): 42–45. Reprinted with permission.

time and the inclination to sit down and show him the industry ropes" (Appelbaum and Evans 1978, p. 2).

A number of facts must be known before actually writing a book. We are fortunate to have two comprehensive studies about academic book authors and text editors to assist us. Robinson and Higbee (1978) and Seligman and Kelly (1990) provide a wealth of information about book writing and the publishing processes from an author's viewpoint. For those who have written one or more books, reading the studies offers a means by which to compare your own experiences to those of others. For beginners, these studies may illustrate where much of your occupational activity may be for the next few years.

The Publishing Industry

Tradebooks and Textbooks

Publishing companies tend to classify books as tradebooks or textbooks. Tradebooks are designed for mass appeal. They cover a variety of topics of general consumer interests and fads, such as aerobics, diets, gardening, home improvements, fiction, nonfiction, science fiction, travel, photography and art, and self-improvement. Textbooks are designed generally for course work offered by schools, training programs, workshops, and seminars. Although books of this nature cover a variety of topics, their content typically is more detailed, sometimes containing in-depth theoretical and philosophical foundations and applied uses, and is often written in technical terms for occupationally specialized target audiences.

Publisher distinctions like these usually are moot for academic authors. The distinction that is more important, especially for beginning authors, is whether a commercial publisher, university press, professional association/organization publisher, or vanity press is selected. Each type operates in a different environment and with different expectations and required standards for authors.

Commercial Publishers

Commercial publishers are in business primarily to earn a profit for their boards and stockholders. In recent years many of the larger commercial publishers have been purchased by multimedia communication corporations (Graburn 1981). According to Nelson (1978), many large publishing houses generate more than 100 books annually, employ full-time artists and designers, print thousands of copies of each book, and market their products either to the impulse-buy trade or specialty trade. Commercial publishers have lower direct costs per copy, higher mark-up prices, and a lower than average discount. The discount may be for volume or for sales purposes. Most commercial publishers print academic and scholarly works as well as strictly commercial books and do press runs twice as long as is common for most university press books (Morton 1980, p. 364).

Textbooks make up the most frequently published works within the academic and scholarly book category among commercial publishers. High-volume sales textbooks in undergraduate courses generate considerable revenue for these companies. Every field, for example, has one or two "classics" that are at or past their third edition. Instructors often order the current edition of a book for their classes that they once used as students. Since the academic niche was filled so successfully years ago by these books, few academicians believe it necessary to attempt the uphill task of producing and marketing a rival. The original authors of such classics simply continue to update their books at the request of their publishers.

Commercial publishers also attempt to capture part of a large portion of existing or potential consumers through aggressive marketing and possibly by offering subsidies to authors or purchasers in hopes of developing a classic textbook. Usually the focus is geared to meeting the textbook needs of introductory courses. Occasionally companies concentrate on specific fields or areas in an attempt to develop a reputation for publishing certain types of books (medical, law, social sciences). Such a reputation simply increases the likelihood that students and professionals in those chosen fields will focus their purchasing on one or two publishers.

Finally, commercial publishers also may include other specialty categories, such as "first-of-a-kind" books that report new techniques, innovative practices, discoveries, social trends, and legislative mandates and interpretations. Any subject matter that is anticipated to be highly marketable through bookstores, to libraries, or to the general public will be attractive to commercial publishers.

University Presses

University presses generally limit their publishing activities to scholarly and academic works. They have a long and distinguished tradition dating to their origin at Oxford University in 1478 (Meyer and Phillabaum 1980). A university press was first established in the United States 400 years later at The Johns Hopkins University. Almost "without exception scholars hold university presses in high regard" (Ward 1984, p. 33). Some of that esteem may emanate from the fact that university presses have not focused principally on marketability as the criterion for publishing books. Producing hallmark works instead has been their goal.

Maintaining this standard of excellence, unfortunately, has contributed to financial problems for many university presses. Because the publishing process is lengthy, the direct costs high for complex and comprehensive texts, and the return on investment low in terms of sales of highly priced works, university presses seldom make substantial profits (Mills 1983). Those few that manage to stay solvent are regarded highly among academic authors, publishers, and university administrators. Given the long-term endurance and tradition of universities' and their presses' consistency, stability, and indeed the survival of the university press will rise or fall with the fate of scholarship and higher education. Simply put "university presses are the most efficient means yet devised to putting scholarship into print," especially those materials "that commercial houses would not normally risk publishing" (Sutherland 1990, pp. 88–89). The miniboom, the growing need for teachers, and other factors bode well for the future of university presses (Bailey 1988).

Given that "fully one book in six in print today bears a university press imprint" attests to the impact of these sources (Meyer and Phillabaum 1980, p. 218). With the realization that many commercial houses have "become mere printers rather than publishers" (Graburn 1981, p. 76) and that many university presses publish materials where the intention is to "bridge the gaps that sometimes appear between the academic community and society as a whole" (Meyer and Phillabaum 1980, p. 214), the actual impact of these presses is considerable.

Due to these increasing financial difficulties, however, most university presses now publish some marketable popular books, like cookbooks, to offset the cost of printing substantive works for limited audiences. Financial problems have forced university presses to reduce the number of hardback books they produce by 22 percent (Smith 1977). The trend today is to require more author involvement in production, such as asking authors to provide manuscripts on computer disks. Such procedures, currently used by commercial publishers, are being adopted by university presses without sacrificing the quality historically associated with them. Nevertheless, these changes place a greater burden on press staff and authors. Authors now must be more involved in the entire publishing operation instead of simply writing manuscripts and proofreading galleys. Along with more responsibilities, however, authors acquire more information about the book-publishing process and are better able to assist with layout, setup, design, and marketing.

Association/Organizational Publishers

Association/organizational publishers sometimes border on the academic publishing arena. Association publishing generally represents a project by members of a group for their membership. Publications such as these are rarely reviewed by publishing professionals and in fact sometimes are not reviewed at all. There are isolated fields, however, wherein monographs and books are produced by extremely specialized literary or learned societies. According to McKeon (1983), the essence of association publishing is twofold: "Hard-bound books reflect effort and research, much more so than a brochure or paper-bound book" and "publishing a book can give an association executive an excellent public relations tool, a prime gift item, a memento of a major event, and a severe headache" (p. 79).

Vanity Presses

Vanity presses exist principally for authors who wish to pay a printer to transform a written manuscript into a book (i.e., setup, layout, typesetting, printing, and binding). An alternative to vanity presses is the do-it-yourself approach. "You get bids from three or four printers, decide on the quantity you want to print, and find somewhere to warehouse the product" (Mager 1986, p. 117). Vanity presses offer no review of the materials, no editing other than that performed by the author, no evaluation of the accuracy or thoroughness of the material, no assessment of the work's quality, in short no quality control. This appraisal essentially expresses the impact such works have on their fields and within academia.

Preparing Proposals

There are quite a number of considerations for preparing effective book proposals. Some of these are contained in Table 6.1 and Figure 8.1. According to Baker (1982), who has twenty-seven books to his credit, "you must appeal to the editor's self-interest in finding a book that is profit-making" (p. 8). This advice has other connotations as far as university presses are concerned, however. Such things as uniqueness, novelty, scholarly nature, status, and visibility could be considered "profit-making" by a university press.

Another tip Baker suggests is to "become the editor reading, not the author writing" (p. 9). Put yourself in the editor's position and try to conceptualize how that person examines your proposal, comparing it to the stack of others awaiting review. A helpful hint is to examine publisher guides to authors. Printed for distribution by publishers, these brief guides are sent to authors usually after a book contract is signed, but often it is possible to obtain one beforehand. Like earlier cited guides from professional organizations and journal guidelines for contributors, publisher guides specify format requirements to which manuscripts must conform.

According to Oberrecht (1985), "page one is the most important part of an outline; it is where you hook or lose editors" (p. 21). From an editor's perspective, this means receiving a neat, clean, well-constructed, proofread, errorless, and compelling proposal. Don't forget, editors like originals typed or printed on paper with rag content — it has the feel of quality. Remember that the "proposal is the sales tool you take to your publisher" (Sonnesyn 1989, p. 17); it must be professional in all respects.

Table 6.1 also mentions the simultaneous submission of manuscripts. Although this point was raised earlier, it deserves reiteration. Hogan and Cohen (1965) cite that "many university presses will not look at a manuscript that is being considered elsewhere" (p. 33). It is wise, therefore, to speak with other authors who have worked with the publisher you are considering or simply call the editor to discover the

---

BOOK PROPOSAL CHECKLIST

Cover letter
____ Is it short and simple?
____ Does it introduce you and your proposal?
____ Does it avoid items examined in depth in the proposal?
____ Is the letter neat, clean, proofed, and correct (as the entire proposal must be)?
____ Have you indicated that the proposal is being sent to other publishers?

Title
____ Is the title wholly descriptive?
____ Does the title have eye appeal?
____ Have you provided alternate titles?
____ Have you examined the titles of similar books?

Scope of book
____ Have you briefly stated the focus/purpose of the book?
____ Did you indicate why it is innovative? new? novel?
____ Are all the unique characteristics explained?

Audience
____ Have you adequately described the intended/potential audience?
____ Did you list fields, areas of study, professions, etc., to whom it will appeal?
____ Are courses and perhaps schools who would use/buy the book indicated?

Marketing
____ Have you indicated why this will sell?
____ Did you provide evidence for why you think this will sell "X" copies in three to five years?
____ Did you explain how you will help? Did you list appropriate journals, associations, and their newsletters for ads?
____ Is a list of professionals who will help market/push in their schools possible?
____ Do you have mailing lists/labels for flyers/brochures?
____ Are you aware that much of the marketing depends on you and your knowledge of the field and its resources?
____ Are you willing to appear on television or radio and travel to promote the book?

Biographical sketch
____ Why are you qualified to write this book?
____ How do they know you will do it and do it well within guidelines and deadlines?
____ Is a vita/resume attached?
____ Other authors, who are they?
____ Have publications by all authors been noted?

Chapters
____ Is a neat, clean, totally completed first chapter included?
____ Are two or three other chapters, not drafts/rough, also submitted?
____ Will the editor see/read enough to really know what you propose?
____ Have you provided an outlined table of contents? Is it in outline form for the entire book?
____ Do you have chapter-by-chapter outlines?

Time
____ What completion date did you give? Did you multiply your best estimate by a factor of two to four?
____ What portion/percentage of the work is completed?
____ At what stage are you now on the project?

Extras
____ How did you describe illustrations/figures? Did you include some completed printer-ready items?
____ Have you expressed your familiarity with camera-ready/printer-ready materials?
____ Will copyright releases be involved? Do you already have them?
____ Do you intend to do the index?
____ Have you discussed this with a publisher's representative who visited campus or is nearby?

Figure 8.1. Book proposal checklist.

publisher's policy. In the event these suggestions are not taken, however, at least do not fail to indicate simultaneous submission in the cover letter to the editor.

No matter how well you follow these steps and hints, book publishers often take an inordinate amount of time to make decisions. Sattelmeyer (1989) recounts a case of a scholar who spent five years writing his second book. Submitting it to his first publisher, at their request, he received his last initial review in nine months. Two revisions and five readers' reports later no contract decision had been made. After five years of writing, four years of editorial review, and one year in production the book was printed (p. 174).

As a second example, *Persist and Publish* was sent to several commercial and university presses. Within six months we received a contract from one of them which after examination we decided not to accept because the publisher offered neither a review nor editorial suggestions. Shortly afterward we received a telephone call expressing interest from the University Press of Colorado. During the same month we received another contract offer by telephone and serious letters of interest from two other publishers. Some publishers simply never responded with even an acknowledgement of receipt. The bottom line for us was to sign with the best publisher, who, by their efficiency, showed genuine interest. This method also revealed to us a hint of how efficient the publisher might be in the future with galleys, page proofs, manufacturing, and marketing.

Contract Negotiations

With the exception of law school faculty, others in academia usually lack specific knowledge necessary to truly understand important aspects of a contract. Suffice it to say, most book contracts are written in legalese. The best advice for beginning authors is to thoroughly read the contract. If questions arise about the mutual and respective responsibilities of each party (author and publisher), default conditions and penalties, and other terms of the agreement, ask the editor. Although there are usually some controversies or questions involved in contracts, when authors perform good-faith efforts to meet their responsibilities, publishers will do so as well (Caute and Graham 1983; McQuaid 1982).

Most problems encountered with publishers generally occur when authors fail to meet deadlines, do not follow submission guidelines and requirements, or refuse to accept reasonable editorial or copyediting suggestions. However, if the language and terms of contracts continue to be confusing even after the new writer has consulted with experienced authors, the new author should seek the advice of an attorney. An attorney can explain the issues and terms involved clause by clause. Before consulting an attorney, however, the new author should make every effort to seek clarification from the editor assigned to handle the book.

Working With Editors

Nothing can improve a book more than an experienced, involved, and caring editor. Because both parties desire to communicate a message as clearly as possible and to publish the best book possible, a good relationship between both author and editor enhances the entire publishing process (Mann 1981). Such a relationship has the potential to be an ideal learning collaboration for those concerned. Although beginning writers will have more to learn, editors usually gain considerable knowledge about writers' fields of interest during the editorial process.

One approach to facilitating writer-editor relationships is to examine some of the problems editors have experienced. Among the most frequent are when authors "won't really try, [when they] are careless in copying quotes, [and when they] fail to clarify or simplify . . . so many errors that their data and conclusions become suspect" (Denham and Broom 1981, p. 249). Sometimes editors must deal with authors who seem to believe that their academic position carries with it an ability to write flawlessly.

Editors must be concerned with potential sales, even for scholarly books, especially to people who could appreciate a work without necessarily being trained in the author's specific discipline. Tables and figures that only appeal to or are understood by a handful of potential readers, however, are likely to be eliminated. Another example that gives editors the impression that some authors are careless is when names and dates cited in the text do not correspond to those in the reference or bibliography section. Finally, editors become particularly upset when authors miss deadlines.

Authors have complaints about editors as well. Mansbridge (1980) reports the three most frequent irritants are excessive copyediting, poor communication, and failure of editors to provide assistance. Although most author complaints appear to represent unmet expectations about the editorial and review processes, perhaps the basis of the problem lies with the reasonableness of the expectations. If a copy editor is changing quotations, essential words, or integral phrases, then authors must resist editorial modifications. "There is a saying among editors that a good copy editor does not leave footprints in a manuscript" (Van Til 1986, p. 276). Once again, such matters should be discussed and clarified with the editor before any other actions are taken (in haste or through avoidance) by authors.

The path to effective communication and collaboration between editors and authors can have its potholes nevertheless. Sometimes it seems that editors and authors have an especially difficult time simply contacting each other. For example, when telephone messages and letters seem to go unanswered, or are delayed for long periods, it is not uncommon for people to feel they are being ignored. The problem in truth may be that each party's personal and work schedules do not coincide. Before allowing inconveniences to become a barrier to developing an effective working relationship, remember several things:

- Editors rarely work with only one author, just as academic writers seldom are assigned only one student to advise.
- You should keep a log or file of calls, letters, and other attempts to contact the editor.
- If unanswered questions begin interfering with meeting agreed-upon deadlines, write the director or editor-in-chief of the publishing firm, making certain to send a copy to the editor assigned to your manuscript.
- Authors tend to think a book is finished when it is written. Editors know that the work has just begun when a manuscript is submitted.

```
AUTHOR:

TITLE:

READER:

            SOUTHERN ILLINOIS UNIVERSITY PRESS
                    READER'S REPORT

(For the reader's information:  Please be frank in your
opinion.  Your name will not be revealed to the author of this
manuscript without your permission.  The Press and the author
will be grateful to you for any suggestions for revision you
care to offer.  Please add extra sheets to this form as
required.)

Is this manuscript a contribution to its field?  How important
is the field?


What is the nature and scope of the audience addressed?


Is the organization of the book sound?


Is the style adequate to the purpose of the book?


Are the author's techniques sound?


If you were a publisher of scholarly books, would you consider
this manuscript a worthy addition to your list?


Are there competing books in the field?


My final reaction to this manuscript is that I (would) (would
not) publish it.

REMARKS:


                            _____
                                      Signature


_____      _____
       Date                            Address

This report is confidential.  Your name will not be revealed to
the author of the manuscript unless specifically in your
remarks you have included permission to reveal it.
```

Figure 8.2a. Sample manuscript reader's report. Reprinted with permission from Southern Illinois University Press.

```
AUTHOR:

TITLE:

READER'S NAME:

READER'S AFFILIATION:

                    STATE UNIVERSITY OF NEW YORK PRESS

                              READER'S REPORT

1.   Is the manuscript competently written?  Is the scholarship sound?  Is it accurate?  Is the
     organization good?  Do the conclusions follow from the evidence?  If the answer to any one of
     these questions is negative, please simply write "NO" and indicate the problems on a separate
     sheet.  These are qualifications for further consideration.

         YES       NO

2.   What do you like most about this manuscript?

3.   What is your greatest concern about this manuscript?

4.   Is the manuscript interesting to read?

5.   Is the topic significant?  Is it important in itself or central to an important field of study?

6.   Is this work useful?  Would the book be useful enough that a reasonable number of individual
     persons (not libraries) would buy it?

7.   Does the author show unsuspected ramifications, provide insights and flashes of recognition, and
     bring forth something of intellectual importance in the texture of the work?

8.   What are the competing books in this field if any?

9.   Do you recommend publication of this manuscript?

         YES       NO

Additional Comments:

Please rank this manuscript on the following scale:

A.   Outstanding..._____                          Home address:_____
B.   Excellent....._____                          _____
C.   Good.........._____
D.   Average......._____                          Social Security #_____
E.   Acceptable...._____
                                                   _____
F.   Unpublishable._____                                   (Signature)

_____                    _____
          (Date)                                            (Place)

This report is confidential.  Your name will not be revealed to the author of the manuscript unless
specifically in your remarks you have included permission to reveal it.
```

Figure 8.2b. Sample manuscript reader's report. Reprinted with permission from State University of New York Press.

Finally, several authors have noted that the trend is toward giving many previous editorial responsibilities to authors (Luey 1989; Pascal 1982; Sikula 1979). Certainly the trend gives authors more control over the final product than in years past. Howe (1982) suggests that authors seriously consider working with independent professional editors in conjunction with the publisher's assigned editor especially when: (1) you do not receive the kind of assistance expected from publishers, (2) participation in marketing and advertising the book are desired, (3) close supervision and control are desired in cover design, art work, layout, and copy editing, and (4) you want to learn about the academic publishing process. When using an independent editor, however, it is crucial to give the independent editor all the manuscript guidelines provided by the publisher and inform the publisher that the submitted manuscript has passed the scrutiny of an independent professional editor.

Seeking New Challenges
in the Publishing Game

Writing and publishing hold more rewards than simply the enjoyment of seeing your name in print. Sikula (1979) points out that publishing helps establish one's credibility in a chosen profession. Academic writing and publishing also provide opportunities to explore different styles of written self-expression. The purpose of this chapter is to examine some of these alternate outlets. In order to accomplish this, this chapter contains four sections: (1) idea catalysts, (2) book reviews, (3) editorial appointments, and (4) nonacademic writing.

Idea Catalysts

Ideas are the foundation upon which human endeavors are based. The "idea" to write this book, for example, was prompted by many observations, experiences, attitudes, values, beliefs, and possible rewards, as well as a tangible answer to the question, "Why not?" However, an idea does not amount to much if its originator is unwilling to carry it forth through some kind of action. The idea alone to write this book did not get the job done. Motivation, perseverance, enthusiasm, and particularly the physical activity of writing certainly helped in getting the idea into concrete form. This may be interesting to some people, but the question of where or how one conjures ideas remains unanswered. Perhaps there is no simple or single answer, but experience has revealed many idea catalysts for academic writing.

For new academics, almost any behavior that may lead to writing for publication should be encouraged. Alley and Cargill (1986) mention several activities that seem to enhance generating ideas as well as increasing your visibility and reputation in your profession: (1) attend professional meetings, (2) volunteer for committee work, (3) write letters to editors, and (4) establish personal contacts. Three other activities also are worth considering: (1) observation, (2) assimilation, and (3) evaluation. These activities aid in generating an abundance of ideas that in turn will lead to more ideas being generated.

By attending professional meetings, you may learn about current and future trends in your chosen occupation. These trends may become the topics about which writers will want to write. By volunteering for and interacting with committees and task forces, you may exchange information with other attendees, brainstorm new possibilities and solutions, and make new acquaintances and friendships for subsequent contact and collaborative efforts. According to Walker (1978), it is only through conferring and corresponding that you eventually will be on a first-name basis with journal editors, noted authors, and other luminaries in your field. For example, a congratulatory note to a newly appointed editor you met at a conference may lead to the idea of nominating you when new editorial advisory board members are sought.

Take advantage of every opportunity to become known and to write. This is where it is especially important to be ever mindful to observe, assimilate, and evaluate. Listen to what is said in your field by colleagues as well as to what is said about your field by those outside it. Become aware of interrelationships between your chosen field and others, even those that are perceived by your colleagues as tangential at best. Finally, assess the relationships between your surroundings, other fields, and what you know about your profession. You might be surprised at the volume of ideas that emerge about which you could be the first to draft a manuscript.

If this advice seems rather vague, perhaps some of the examples below will be more illustrative of a seemingly endless variety of idea prompters:

1. How do technologies affect your occupation?
2. What are the social influences that affect your occupation?

3. Does your occupation influence society? If so, how?
4. What skills of your occupation are also those of other fields?
5. Do personal computers really increase your work efficiency?
6. Do the clothes you wear affect the way others act toward you? How does their apparel influence you?
7. How does the national or world economy affect your field?
8. How will space travel/technology affect your occupation?
9. Does "flex time" improve the output of your job?
10. How do people outside of your field perceive your job?
11. Are supervisor's expectations of your job congruent with the actual job requirements?

Book Reviews

"On an edition of 2000 copies . . . a publisher may send out 100 complimentary copies for review" (MacPhail 1980, p. 57). While such a number of "free" copies may seem extravagant to most readers, it makes economic sense for a publishing company. A hundred complimentary copies mailed to selected scholars who may require the book for their classes, for example, has a greater potential return on investment for a fraction of the cost of several advertisements in professional media publications. Those who benefit most from the copies are academicians who are beginning their writing careers, because a "free" book may require a written review for periodicals and journals.

Denham (1982) advises that "the single best way to get started in publishing . . . is to write book reviews" (p. 203). Writing book reviews offers a number of advantages for those who are beginning to develop writing habits, for those who want to expand their range of publications, or for those who want to begin building a scholarly reputation. One advantage is that journal editors are usually quite eager to find professionals who can write reviews reasonably quickly and efficiently. Figure 9.1 provides an example of how actively journal editors seek competent book reviewers.

Another advantage to writing book reviews is the attention they receive from subscribers who may be eager to find new materials and resources, but who have insufficient time and finances to review the

---

Reviewers Welcomed

R ehabilitation professionals who have an interest in writing feature book reviews for this section should so inform the Associate Editor, *Rehabilitation Literature*, 2023 W. Ogden Avenue, Chicago, Illinois 60612. Please include a vita sheet and specify the areas of interest you may have so that we will be able to provide you with an appropriate selection should you be asked to write a review.

Figure 9.1a. Call for book reviewers. From *Rehabilitation Literature* 46(9–10): 289. Reprinted with permission.

What's New in 1989

As you have already noticed by our expanded Table of Contents, our inside cover, and the heading at the top of this page, something has happened to your old favorite, the Audiovisual Reviews section. Responding to libraries' needs and demands for more and better video and audio services, we are separating the two sections and expanding each to cover more programs. As such, Video Reviews and Audio Reviews are looking for a few good reviewers. Covering more programs means more media specialists and librarians are needed to contribute their expertise. Don't let the decade end without becoming a part of our review team. In addition, we now have the capability of receiving reviews via computer. So if returning to your old Smith-Corona kept you from reviewing all these years, *LJ* has entered the technological age. If you are interested in reviewing videocassettes (VHS or U-matic) and/or audiocassettes, send a writing sample to Bette-Lee Fox, Audio/Video Reviews, *Library Journal*, 249 W. 17 Street, New York, NY 10011.

Figure 9.1b. Call for book reviewers. From *Library Journal* 114(1): 110. Reprinted with permission.

materials themselves. Book reviews seldom undergo the same blind, refereed examination characteristic of article manuscripts. Although some periodicals scrutinize reviews quite seriously, standards for publication generally are less rigorous and frequently at the discretion of a book review editor or the journal editor (Hoge and West 1979). Feedback provided by the book review or journal editor offers invaluable information to novice writers about improving writing style and an opportunity to learn the publishing process and to make important contacts in publishing circles.

In addition to responding to calls for book reviewers, some experts propose contacting journal editors to indicate an interest in writing reviews in specific areas. When making such an offer, however, it is wise to enclose a review of a book in your field. "Thus, for the price of a stamp, you [may] get a book for free and a chance to get published" (Dorn 1980, p. 408). The only potential drawback with this suggestion is that the majority (55.2 percent) of journal editors do not accept unsolicited reviews (Budd 1982). Nevertheless, the odds for publication (i.e., 44.8 percent) seem to favor taking the risk.

Winning publication of unsolicited reviews can be enhanced further based on suggestions by Klemp (1981) and Woodring (1982). Generally, there are two kinds of book reviews. One form resembles a table of contents wherein each chapter and section thoroughly examined and critiqued. The other method is a global approach whereby the entire content is reviewed in terms of coverage, credibility, manner of presentation, usefulness, and so forth. Another important tip about writing book reviews is knowing the intended audience of the journal by examining its stated purpose and the interests represented by its readership. The review should clearly illustrate for the audience those features of the text that are important and useful for the readers.

Editorial Appointments

Manuscript Reviews

Journal editors look for reviewers constantly, as illustrated in Figure 9.2. An excellent way to learn about academic writing is by reviewing and analyzing manuscripts that have been submitted for publication consideration. It has been estimated that authors read

---

NOMINATIONS FOR EDITORIAL BOARD AND CONSULTING
REVIEWER POSITIONS

Applications are invited for positions on the RCB Editorial Board, with 3-year terms beginning on July 1, 1986. Professional writing and publication histories of applicants, along with previous manuscript review experience, are the primary selection criteria.
Applications are also invited for positions as Consulting Reviewers. Those appointed will be asked to review up to four manuscripts during their 1-year terms. Professional experience in rehabilitation counseling is a primary selection criterion, although academic credentials are also considered.
Individuals interested in Editorial Board or Consulting Reviewer positions should send a letter of application and vita to the Editor at the address on the inside front cover by May 15, 1986.

Figure 9.2a. Call for journal manuscript reviewers. From *Rehabilitation Counseling Bulletin* 29 (3): 157. Reprinted with permission.

GUEST REVIEWERS FOR VOLUME 21

The contributions of the following Guest Reviewers in reviewing manuscripts, used in conjunction with the reviews of Board members, are gratefully acknowledged:

Beatrice Baldwin
Southeastern Louisiana University

Rich Blake
University of Nebraska at Omaha

Joan Brizzi
Northeastern Ohio Universities

Nina Brown
Old Dominion University

Joseph Ciechalski
East Carolina University

J. Linward Doak
Eastern Kentucky University

Kimberly Hays
University of Illinois at Urbana

Shari Just
Oklahoma State University

L. Scott Lissner
Adelphi University

Peter Manzi
Monroe Community College

Jane Myers
University of Florida

Charles Ryan
Indiana University of Pennsylvania

Terence Tracey
University of Illinois at Urbana

Members, including advanced graduate students, who wish to serve as Guest Reviewers should submit vitae to the Editor and indicate areas of expertise.

Figure 9.2b. Call for journal manuscript reviewers. From *Measurement and Evaluation in Counseling and Development* 21(2): 30. Reprinted with permission.

Members of Underrepresented Groups:
Reviewers for Journal Manuscripts Wanted

If you are interested in reviewing manuscripts for APA journal, the APA Publications and Communications Board would like to invite your participation. Manuscript reviewers are vital to the publication process. As a reviewer, you would gain valuable experience in publishing. The P&C Board is particularly interested in encouraging members of underrepresented groups to participate in this process.

If you are interested in reviewing manuscripts, please write to Leslie Cameron at the address below. Please note the following important points:

*To be selected as a reviewer, you must have published articles in peer-reviewed journals. The experience of publication provides a reviewer with the basis for preparing a thorough, objective evaluative review.
*To select the appropriate reviewers for each manuscript, the editor needs detailed information. Please include with your letter your vita. In your letter, please identify which APA journal you are interested in and describe your area of expertise. Be as specific as possible. For example, "social psychology" is not sufficient—you would need to specify "social cognition" or "attitude change" as well.
*Reviewing a manuscript takes time. If you are selected to review a manuscript, be prepared to invest the necessary time to evaluate the manuscript thoroughly.

Write to Leslie Cameron, Journals Office, APA, 1400 N. Uhle Street, Arlington, Virginia 22201.

Figure 9.2c. Call for journal manuscript reviewers. From *Professional Psychology: Research and Practice* 19(3): 297. Reprinted with permission of the American Psychological Association.

nearly 100 times the amount they write in order to become conversant with the topics presented in their manuscripts (Zirkel 1978). Serving as a manuscript reviewer assists in the process of information gathering, as well as evaluating the thoroughness of materials submitted by others. Obviously, the more you are perceived as knowledgeable about a particular field of study, the greater the likelihood of being selected as a reviewer.

When openings or searches occur to fill vacancies on editorial boards or reviewer positions, novice writers should send a letter expressing interest and a willingness to participate. "In the letter you should describe or label three to six specific subareas of research that you feel particularly well qualified to review" (Eichorn and VandenBos 1985, p. 1316). It is wise to repeat this process each time such an announcement appears, just in case you are not selected initially.

For practical purposes, do not expect to be selected as a reviewer or editorial board member initially if you are a novice writer. At this point in your career, it is important to convey your interest and willingness by responding to such announcements repeatedly. By doing so, editorial selection panels become familiar with your name, educational and experiential backgrounds, and perhaps most importantly, your desire and interest to be involved. Furthermore, your efforts may result in an initial assignment as a consulting or ad hoc reviewer. These consulting or ad hoc assignments generally are acknowledged annually in the last issue of a volume series. Time, experience, publications, and credible reviews will enhance your chances for being invited eventually to become a regular member of the journal's editorial board.

If you are fortunate enough to be selected as a reviewer, several tips are worthy of consideration.

1. Remember and consider the manuscript rejections you may have received. Use them as a model in terms of how their suggestions provided guidance for revisions you were asked to make.
2. Be courteous in your comments. Avoid personal criticisms directed to the author(s).
3. If the manuscript fails to follow the journal's adopted format, consider suggesting that the author(s) have a professional typist prepare the revision.
4. Avoid ambiguous comments that provide little guidance, such as "too long," "unclear," or "I don't agree."
5. Provide specific suggestions such as, "Perhaps the author(s) should examine the enclosed article that deals with the issue being addressed."
6. Finally, remember to review and return the manuscript promptly to the editor. If unable to meet the editor's requested deadline, however, return the manuscript and review forms immediately along with a letter of explanation.

Commentary Reviews

A form of publishing that resembles book reviews is the invited commentary. Journals that use commentaries do so as an additional

CALL FOR COMMENTORS

The *Journal of Rehabilitation Administration* needs persons willing to serve as "Commentors" for articles accepted for publication. Comments are published with the article.

The purpose of the comments section is to focus on the implications of an article's information, particularly for practitioners. Attention is given to identifying ways in which the article provides practical assistance to managers. Commentors may incorporate a creative extension and/or critique of the concepts or content of an article.

If interested, send a letter briefly indicating your major areas of background and interest to:

James A. Bitter, *JRA* Editor
College of Business Administration
University of Northern Colorado
Greeley, Colorado 80639

Figure 9.3. Call for journal article commentors. From *Journal of Rehabilitation Administration* 13(3): 112. Reprinted with permission.

form of review, assessment, and opinion of the articles that are published. Commentaries usually are written by invited practitioners (nonacademics) for their experiential perspective, although it is not uncommon for academically oriented professionals to be asked for their views in such a forum. Commentaries generally appear after the articles about which they are written.

Although commentaries and manuscript reviews share some common characteristics, many important features differentiate the two. Unlike manuscript reviews, commentaries are written after a paper has been accepted for publication. In other words, the manuscript already has successfully completed the blind refereed process. Commentaries are written with full knowledge of the author's identity, and vice versa. They are similar to book reviews in that both are usually reviewed by the editor and/or associate editor(s) prior to publication, instead of blind referees. Unlike manuscript reviews, commentaries may require rewriting because their goal is to achieve publication along with the article. Because they are reviewed and printed, commentaries are considered to be evidence of academic publication, although they receive less merit weight than published articles.

```
                    SPECIAL VOLUME ON SPORT AND THE ARTS
                          CALL FOR CONTRIBUTIONS

    The editors of QUEST, the journal of the National Association of Physical
Education in Higher Education, are planning a special issue devoted entirely to
sport and the arts. The issue will include works of poetry, art and photography
that deal specifically with sport, exercise and human movement.
    Poetry, black and white photographs, and works of art rendered camera ready
for black and white reproduction, clearly identified as to author, should be
submitted in triplicate with captions typewritten on a separate sheet. Each
visual submission may be accompanied by brief commentary not to exceed 250
words. A group or series of visual illustrations related to a single theme may
be accompanied by an extended commentary not to exceed 250 words per
illustration.
    All submissions will be reviewed by a special panel appointed for this issue.
Bruce Noble will serve as guest editor for the volume. Submissions,
postmarked not later than February 15, 1989, should be mailed to Dr. Bruce
Noble, PEHRS Department, 117 Lambert Gym, Purdue University, West
Lafayette, IN 47907, (317) 494-3178. Inquiries regarding the issue should be
mailed to Dr. Noble. An attempt will be made to return all materials submitted
in connection with this issue, whether published or not. Authors are encouraged
to include a self addressed envelope with sufficient postage to cover return
mailing. QUEST cannot assume responsibility for safe return of materials.
```

Figure 9.4a. Call for special issue manuscripts: sport and the arts. From *Journal of Sport History* 15(2): 233. Reprinted with permission.

Finally, commentaries are intended to be critical appraisals of published articles. However, it is very important to remember that the critiqued articles have received expert, blind review by selected referees and have been deemed publishable. If the commentary infers that the manuscript should not have been accepted for publication, or is deficient in some substantial aspect, the underlying challenge is not to the article's author(s), but directed instead to the journal's editor, associate editor, and referees. Furthermore, if the commentary is especially critical of an article's content, rationale, or methodology, the journal's editor may send a copy of the commentary (prior to publication) to the article's author(s) for an invited rejoinder that will appear with the commentary. In one such episode, the author's printed reply simply thanked the seven professionals who approved the article for publication, citing their extensive educational and experiential backgrounds, and thanked the commentary writer for the courtesy of at least reading the article.

Calls for Manuscripts

Calls for manuscripts occur with great regularity for a variety of reasons. Their goal is to increase reader participation by seeking

Call For Manuscripts - Special Issue
Rehabilitation Counseling with Special Populations: State of the Art

The Fall, 1983 issue of **JARC** will be entitled, "Rehabilitation Counseling with Special Populations: State of the Art." Potential topical areas include but are not limited to the following special populations:

Industrially Injured	**Developmentally Disabled**
Alcoholism	**Cancer**
Cardiovascular Disorder	**Psychiatric Disability**
Physical Disability	**Visual Impairment**
Hearing Impairment	**Spinal Cord Injury**
Pulmonary Dysfunction	**Disorders of Bone and Joints**
Chronic Renal Failure	**Other**

The intent of this special issue is to provide a functional description of the process and practice of rehabilitation counseling as related to the special needs of the various disabling conditions. To ensure consistency of coverage with each population, an outline of suggested content and format will be distributed upon request.

The special issue will be coordinated by two special issue editors. Further information may be obtained from either:

Dr. Dennis R. Maki
N362 Lindquist Center
The University of Iowa
Iowa City, IA

Dr. T.F. Riggar
Rehabilitation Institute
Southern Illinois University
Carbondale, IL

Figure 9.4b. Call for manuscripts: special issue. From the *Journal of Applied Rehabilitation Counseling* 13(3): 5. Reprinted with permission of the National Rehabilitation Association.

Editorial

Measurement and Evaluation in Counseling and Development has a tradition of publishing comprehensive and useful issues on a particular theme. In recent years, there have been the following special issues: "Symposium--Testing for Career Counseling, Guidance, and Education" (July 1982) and "Counseling and Development: Critical Issues in Measurement and Evaluation" (October 1984).

A number of topics are being considered for either special issues or areas in which manuscripts are solicited. These topics are the following:

. Teacher competency
. Counselor competency
. Student competency
. Leadership role of counselors in school testing programs

. Proper and improper preparation for testing
. Assessment for non-English speaking students
. Assessment for students for whom English is a second language
. Assessment in mental health agencies
. Assessment in business and industry
. Marriage and family counseling
. Assessment for international students
. Assessment for disabled students
. Bias in research and assessment
. Issues in evaluation

If you are searching for topics for research or discussion in any of the areas above, please send me your contribution for consideration.

--William E. Sedlacek, Editor

Figure 9.4c. Call for manuscripts: editorial. From *Measurements and Evaluation in Counseling and Development* 1 (1): 2. Reprinted with permission.

A new JRA Feature

"THE MANAGER'S FORUM"

The *Journal of Rehabilitation Administration* invites practitioners to share management issues, concerns, and innovations in the practice of administration, management and supervision in a wide variety of human service settings. Dialogue and debate among practitioners and responses to *JRA* articles also are encouraged.

Submit manuscripts of one to four double-spaced typed pages. Three copies are requested. Manuscripts will be given an editorial review.

Send manuscripts to the *JRA* Forum Editor:

Steven E. Simon, Ph.D., *JRA* Forum Editor
Chief, Vocational Rehabilitation and Counseling Division
VA Regional Office, MDP 28
1240 East 9th Street
Cleveland, Ohio 44199

Figure 9.4d. Call for manuscripts: the manager's forum. From *Journal of Rehabilitation Administration* 13(3): 114. Reprinted with permission.

information from practitioners, scholars, and students who have something to say but never thought of themselves as publishable authors. Sometimes calls for manuscripts are used to assemble annual monographs and feature issues covering specialized topics and/or to fill space available in journals that have an insufficient number of accepted manuscripts for an issue to go to press. There are four types of manuscripts that do not fit neatly in this section, however, but should be mentioned briefly nevertheless: (1) special issue manuscripts, (2) journal manuscripts, (3) literary contests, and (4) in-brief manuscripts.

Calls for special issue manuscripts are similar to the example presented in Figure 9.4. As technology increases, our need for more specialized information grows. Sometimes technological advances create fields of expertise and practice that were unknown as few as five years ago, or will develop into areas that are not imagined today. At the same time, advances in technology sometimes render previous knowledge and practice obsolete. When such events occur (or seem to be on the horizon), professional journals frequently devote entire issues to examine the phenomena. Calls for manuscripts that address specialized topics seek experts to inform target audiences about the relevant issues.

These situations provide prime opportunities for novice writers to start their publication records. Under these circumstances, it is not uncommon for "guest editors" to be invited by a journal's editor to orchestrate the issue (contact potential authors, select reviewers, establish a prescribed format and/or content for manuscripts to follow, arrange the order of manuscript presentation, and write the editorial). This is a time when your network of contacts in the profession begins to yield dividends. On the one hand, you may be requested by the guest editor(s) to submit a manuscript or serve as a guest reviewer. On the other hand, if a special issue addresses your area of interest and/or expertise specifically, your chances for publication are increased because there may be few if any other papers submitted in competition. Moreover, successful publishing in such an issue provides three significant opportunities: (1) greater individualized assistance from the editor(s) to make your paper publishable, (2) intrinsic and external motivation to begin writing for publication, and (3) audience perception that you are indeed the expert which in turn may begin paving the way for more manuscript requests, submissions, or invited presentations.

Calls for journal manuscripts represent a traditional approach for submitting papers for publication. Generally speaking, calls for journal manuscripts signify the presence of a new editor and/or a limited number of articles in reserve for subsequent issues. One of the items in Figure 9.5, for example, appeared shortly after the *Vocational Evaluation and Work Adjustment Bulletin* changed editors and staff and relocated its office (events that occur for many journals approximately every five years). When such moves take place, outgoing editors try to have a sufficient backlog of accepted manuscripts to help the incoming staff with upcoming issues. When the reserve is low, however, or the flow of submitted manuscripts is interrupted by address changes, calls for papers seem to appear more frequently in the affected journal. Obviously, the dilemma confronting any new editor in such a position provides additional opportunity for aspiring authors to publish their works.

Literary contests represent still another opportunity for publication. When considering these possible outlets, however, it is important to determine whether entry is limited to specific groups. Figure 9.6, for example, reveals that the Vocational Evaluation and Work Adjustment Association (VEWAA) contest is restricted to papers submitted

VOCATIONAL EDUCATION JOURNAL

Published by the American Vocational Association
1410 King Street, Alexandria, Virginia 22314 (703) 683-3111

Call for Manuscripts
1987-1988

Manuscripts and manuscript proposals are invited on the themes summarized below and also on non-theme topics of broad interest. This year we would especially like to include coverage of inner city and rural schools, new technology, and industry viewpoints.

August: Annual Teaching Issue
A potpourri of tips and strategies for classroom success. Possible topics: how to motivate students, develop basic skills or employability skills, organize time, manage competency-based instruction, extend the use of computers, evaluate progress, be a good VSO adviser, enlist the help of parents, keep up to date with the local job market, ward off burnout, and others.
Deadline: March 1.

September: Teamwork on Comprehensive Career Guidance
An update on developments nationwide. Possible topics: a national overview of the status of comprehensive programs of career guidance, placement, and counseling; guidelines for a team approach; program standards; outstanding secondary programs, outstanding postsecondary programs; and others.
Deadline: March 15.

October: After the Perkins Act, What?
A timely review of issues before the field as work begins on reauthorization of the Carl Perkins Vocational Education Act, which expires in 1989. The issue will carry a range of perspectives on key policy questions and a summary of the first draft of AVA's position on the new legislation. Manuscripts should focus on how vocational education can contribute to the achievement of national goals and what processes will make this possible.
Deadline: April 15.

November/December: Improving Our Image
Expert advice on winning friends for vocational education. Manuscripts and proposals are invited on "the image problem" and practical tips for developing public understanding of vocational education's goals and accomplishments. Possible topics: Making the most of Vocational Education Week, preparing a fact sheet, putting out a good newsletter, writing and placing PSAs, organizing a speakers' bureau, writing feature stories, holding a press conference, using students as goodwill ambassadors, mounting a PR campaign, and others.
Deadline: May 15.

January/February: Rebuilding Lives through Vocational Education
A look at the spectrum of difficult human problems that vocational education is helping to solve. In addition to an article on the personal and societal effects of opening careers to people with special needs, we are looking for manuscripts on program approaches to specific problems. Possible topics: vocational rehabilitation partnerships; programs that serve individuals who are incarcerated, physically handicapped, mentally impaired, recent immigrants, school dropouts, or teenage mothers; teaching tips for meeting special needs in the classroom. Articles for this issue must have strong human interest and good photo possibilities.
Deadline: July 1.

March: Developing Basic Skills
The integration of math, science and language skills in vocational instruction in various program areas. Possible topics: the place of basic skills in the vocational classroom; broad-scale curriculum revision efforts; vocational programs that meet academic graduation requirements; helping teachers develop a basic-skills perspective; how to work with academic teachers; approaches to the problem of illiteracy.
Deadline: September 1.

April: International Roundup
An update on the current status of vocational education in other nations. Possible topics: vocational education and the world economy; patterns of vocational education in individual nations; comparisons of different national approaches; the international role of American vocational educators.
Deadline: October 1.

May: The State Technical Committees in Action
A report on the efforts and recommendations of state technical committees established under the Perkins Act, with the focus on curriculum. We will need a national overview and accounts of particularly far-reaching recommendations in specific program areas.
Deadline: November 1.

Send *two copies* of your manuscript with a cover letter to Manuscripts Editor, *Vocational Education Journal*, 1410 King St., Alexandria, VA 22314. *Be sure to keep a copy for yourself.* If you want your manuscript returned, enclose a self-addressed, stamped envelope.

Figure 9.5a. Call for journal manuscripts. From *Vocational Education Journal* 62(1): 77. Reprinted with permission of the American Vocational Association.

IN
PREPARATION
FOR
1989

AIDS EDUCATION
AND PREVENTION
An Interdisciplinary Journal
The official publication of the
International Society for AIDS Education

Editor: Francisco S. Sy, M.D., Dr. PH
Associate Professor of Epidemiology,
Director, Carolina AIDS Research
and Education (CARE Project)
University of South Carolina,
School of Public Health

CALL FOR PAPERS

A IDS EDUCATION AND PREVEN-
TION: AN INTERDISCIPLINARY
JOURNAL will serve as a forum
devoted to publication of original contributions, highlighting existing and
theoretical models of AIDS education and
prevention, including their development,
implementation and evaluation. It will
also cover various public health, ethical,
psychosocial, and public policy issues.
AIDS EDUCATION AND PREVENTION is
pertinent for physicians, nurses, public
health professionals, health educators,
psychologists, counselors, social workers,
behavioral scientists, ethicists, school
teachers, policy makers and other researchers and practitioners who are currently involved in the AIDS field.

Papers: Submit 4 copies of a double-
spaced typed manuscript to Dr. Francisco
Sy at: School of Public Health, University
of South Carolina, Columbia, S.C. 29208

SUBSCRIPTION INFORMATION
Volume 1, 4 issues, 1989
ISSN 0899-9546. Cat. #7700

**FIRST ISSUE SCHEDULED
FOR JANUARY 1989**
Individuals: $30   Institutions: $60
Non-Profit AIDS Service
Organizations: $30.00
American Psychological
Association Members: $25.00

Outside the U.S. add $15.00 (includes air
mail delivery)

REQUEST YOUR SAMPLE COPY TODAY — USE COUPON BELOW

GUILFORD PUBLICATIONS, INC.
72 Spring Street, New York, NY 10012
CALL TOLL FREE 1-800-221-3966
In NY and Canada call (212) 431-9800

Name _____

Address _____

City _____ State _____ Zip _____

Bill my:

☐ MasterCard ☐ VISA ☐ AMEX

Please send:

☐ Volume 1 of AIDS EDUCATION AND PREVENTION
(see rates above) Outside the U.S., add $15.00
for shipping.

☐ Instructions for author guidelines

☐ Sample Copy Issue

☐ Payment Enclosed

☐ Institutional Purchase Order Attached

Account # _____

Signature _____ Exp. ___

NOTE: YOU MAY USE A PHOTOCOPY IN PLACE OF THIS COUPON

Figure 9.5b. Call for journal manuscripts. From *AIDS Education and Prevention*. Reprinted with permission of Guilford Publications, Inc., New York, New York.

CALL FOR MANUSCRIPTS

The *Journal of Sport Behavior* is issuing a call for manuscripts dealing with original empirical investigations and theoretical papers relating to studies of social behavior in the areas of games and sport. Studies or innovations which have practical application for the coach or athlete are also accepted.

Essentially, the *Journal of Sport Behavior* is interested in sociological, psychological, anthropological, and related applications to the science of sport.

The *Journal* is published quarterly (March, June, September, and December). Alternate issues will carry major themes of sociology and psychology, respectively.

Manuscripts should be submitted in triplicate and must be prepared to conform to the style and procedure described in the publication manual of the American Psychological Association, Third Edition (1983). Manuscripts must be accompanied by an abstract in both English and French of 200-250 words typed on separate sheets of paper. Where appropriate to the nature of the article, the abstract should contain statements of (a) the problem, (b) the method, (c) the results, and (d) the conclusions. It should provide the reader with the idea and scope of the article and serve for publication of the abstracts.

Manuscripts and all matters pertaining to subscription should be directed to:

Dr. William F. Gilley
Department of HPELS
University of South Alabama
Mobile, AL 36688

Figure 9.5c. Call for journal manuscripts. From *Journal of Sport Behavior.* Reprinted with permission.

VEWAA Announces Literary Contest

This year VEWAA will sponsor a literary contest devoted to students and practitioners. The objective of the contest is to stimulate both students and practitioners to develop articles and in so doing, make a contribution to the literature. Students are those individuals who are presently in an undergraduate or graduate program in rehabilitation or a closely related field. In order to qualify as a practitioner, the individual must have regular contact with clients, either directly or indirectly, and must not be affiliated with a college or university as an educator or trainer. Each manuscript submitted must have only one author, either a student or practitioner. Four categories are being designated: (1) Student - Vocational Evaluation, (2) Student - Work Adjustment, (3) Practitioner - Vocational Evaluation, and (4) Practitioner - Work Adjustment. Plaques will be awarded to the winners in each category during the 1984 NRA Conference and individuals in a runner-up category will be recognized in an honorable mention category.

Manuscripts are being requested that relate directly to the general practice of vocational evaluation or work adjustment in rehabilitation settings. Each manuscript must be designated for one of the four categories listed above with a maximum length of ten double-spaced typewritten pages. Manuscripts will be subjected to a similar peer review process as those submitted to the *VEWAA Bulletin*. In addition, they will be rated on the basis of (a) general interest, (b) innovativeness, (c) importance to the field, and (d) relevance to application in rehabilitation settings. Individuals submitting manuscripts should follow author guidelines found in the *VEWAA Bulletin* and three copies of each manuscript entered must be submitted. First-place manuscripts will be published in the Fall or Winter issues of the *VEWAA Bulletin* and the deadline for submitting manuscripts is May 15, 1984. The VEWAA Publications Committee will coordinate the review process of submitted manuscripts. *Please submit 3 copies of each manuscript* to Dr. Horace W. Sawyer, Department of Rehabilitation Counseling, Box J-175, JHMHC, University of Florida, Gainesville, Florida 32610.

Rehabilitation Counseling & Services Honor Society
Rho Chi Sigma
1984 Literary Award

The Rho Chi Sigma Literary Awards will be presented at the Society's meeting to be held in conjunction with the 1984 National Rehabilitation Association's National Conference. Two Awards of 'Lifetime Membership' and a Certificate will be presented, one to a student member and the other to a person from the general membership. All applicants must be Society members by the submission deadline of July 1, 1984. Original manuscripts submitted for consideration should not be more than 10 typed, double spaced pages. An essay on any topic relevant to rehabilitation will be considered for the awards. The winners will be selected by the members of the Literary Award Committee. Any questions as well as applications should be forwarded to: Dr. T.F. Riggar, Rehabilitation Institute, Southern Illinois University, Carbondale, IL 62901.

Figure 9.6a. Announcement of literary contest. From *Vocational Evaluation and Work Adjustment Bulletin* 17(1): 35. Reprinted with permission.

The Literature Prize Committee of the MARGARET S. MAHLER PSYCHIATRIC RE-SEARCH FOUNDATION is accepting papers to be considered for the 1988 annual prize of $750.00. Papers should deal with clinical, theoretical, or research issues related to Dr. Mahler's concepts of separation-individuation in child development. Pre-published papers may be submitted, provided that they have been published within the year of the Prize. Six copies of the paper should be submitted no later than December 31, 1988, to: Dr. Marjorie Harley, Chairperson, Margaret S. Mahler Literature Prize Committee, 201 St. Martins Rd., Baltimore, MD 21218

Figure 9.6b. Announcement of literary contest. From *The Psychoanalytic Quarterly* 57(2): 295. Reprinted with permission.

The Journal of
REHABILITATION ADMINISTRATION, INC.
Student Manuscript Competition

To enable students to share original thinking pertinent to rehabilitation administration and to reward quality endeavors addressing policy, program, or practice issues in rehabilitation administration.

The winning manuscript will be awarded $200 and published in Vol 15, No. 1. Manuscripts receiving honorable mention will be noted.

The Journal of Rehabilitation Administration, Inc., publishes practice reports, theoretical papers and applied research studies designed to improve the practice of supervision, management and administration in a wide variety of human service settings.

- Open to full-time students with maximum of two authors per manuscript.
- Manuscripts must conform to "Instructions and Guidelines for Authors" published in the *Journal*.
- Manuscripts that are primarily reviews of the literature are *not* appropriate submissions. Originality and/or contribution to the field is expected.

For additional information call or write:

John F. Newman, Ph.D., Past Editor
Institute of Health Administration
Georgia State University
University Plaza
Atlanta, Georgia 30303
(404) 651-2637

William A. Calzaretta, Ph.D., Associate Editor
DePaul University
Department of Rehabilitation Services
243 South Wabash
Chicago, Illinois 60604
(312) 341-8845

DEADLINE JUNE 30, 1990
Submit four manuscript copies to:
Kathy Williams, Director
JRA Student Manuscript Competition, Office of Vocational Rehabilitation, Capital Plaza Tower—9th Floor, Frankfort, Kentucky 40601

Figure 9.6c. Announcement of literary contest. From *Journal of Rehabilitation Administration* 13 (3): 112. Reprinted with permission.

only from students and practitioners in the fields of vocational evaluation or work adjustment, whereas the Rho Chi Sigma contest is restricted to submissions from its membership.

Finally, in-brief manuscripts are only about half the length of regular journal manuscripts. They generally are solicited by editors from practitioners for several reasons. Perhaps the most important reason is to encourage practitioners to share information about applied projects and/or innovative applications that achieve successful outcomes in their work settings. The term "practitioner," however, should not be interpreted to exclude academicians who also may have discovered innovative applied approaches that could benefit others.

Another reason for in-brief articles is literally to fill space that is insufficient to accommodate the length of the average manuscript. By no means is this meant as a disparaging comment about the potential quality and substance of in-brief articles. It simply reiterates the fact that a blank page costs a journal approximately the same amount as one with printed matter.

Nonacademic Writing

Although this book focuses on academic writing and its rewards, nonacademic writing is worth mentioning for several reasons. Earlier chapters stressed the importance of patience, practice, critical examination and evaluation, and rewriting. Writing that is not intended for academic publication provides a useful means for increasing proficiency. Included among nonacademic outlets are letters to friends and relatives, letters and memoranda to colleagues and work-related contacts, "official" communications at work (such as committee reports, minutes of meetings, course syllabi, and class instructions), and recreational writing (such as poetry, short stories, and novels).

Any kind of writing can be used to practice effective communication — an essential requirement of academic writing. Surely "persistence in trying can eventually help one to become a better writer" (Gay and Edgil 1989, p. 461). Although some nonacademic writing outlets can be great sources of inspiration, leisure, and recreation, they are potential sources of intrinsic and extrinsic rewards. Writing letters to friends and relatives, for example, infers interest, sharing, and caring, which often prompts them to take time to write to you. Work-related writing generally accomplishes job responsibilities. When this goal is achieved, job satisfaction usually increases. Recreational writing offers an outlet for creativity, which in turn can help relieve stress and tension, as well as offering personal satisfaction. In addition, recreational writing potentially can expand one's abilities and awaken new interests and sources of rewards.

The point to be made in this brief section is that the possibilities for which writing can be used (and useful) are substantial. But persistence, patience, practice, critical assessment, and rewriting are essential.

What Happens When the Stargazers See You

This book has provided information that is intended to assist writers who wish to become published authors. A measure of the book's usefulness is whether its content provides sufficient guidance to motivate would-be authors to submit manuscripts that result in publications. Assuming that the book achieves its goal, a brief word about notoriety seems to be a fitting conclusion.

Writers who publish attain recognition from their colleagues and members of their field who read its professional journals. Sometimes the substantive qualities of authors' works result in notoriety and recognition extending beyond their professions. This chapter provides information about coping effectively with this type of recognition. Three brief sections offer helpful hints about stars and stargazers, authorities and experts, and command performances.

Stars and Stargazers

Academic authors seldom begin their writing careers with the goal of becoming literary "stars." It is probably safe to say that the majority are responding to a professional obligation to contribute to the literature of their fields and/or to survive in a publish-or-perish environment (see Chapter 2). Regardless of specific motivations, it seems reasonable to assume that published authors become more noticed by their colleagues. Of course the duration and intensity with which authors receive such recognition depend on such factors as the number of their publications and the perceived importance of their writings. Although presidents of professional organizations, academic directors, and state commissioners often achieve the same heights of recognition (see Figure 2.2), that status is frequently fleeting. Publications, especially books, are substantial and enduring. The skills and knowledge necessary to publish are often more respected and admired than the political behaviors needed to attain upper-level leadership positions. Given both factors, it is likely that even in name recognition people who have published works rate higher in overall visibility than do transient elected, appointed, or selected leaders in the field.

As authors acquire increased recognition, their professional stature generally increases as well. Perhaps most of us recall the thrill we felt as students upon meeting the author of one of our textbooks. Such episodes seemed more memorable when the author was regarded as the leading authority in our field, or perhaps more importantly, one of its founders. Certainly the encounter was more enjoyable when we learned that such a significant person seemed to be sincere and friendly. But what would our impression have been if the author had responded some other way? Moreover, what impression did we make with the author?

Encounters between published writers and their readers generally occur in public forums such as conventions, conferences, workshops, and sponsored colloquia. Impressions the stars make on the stargazers, and vice versa, may enhance or hinder subsequent writing careers.

Authorities and Experts

Most professionals strive to become experts, and later a few are recognized as authorities. There exists a subtle yet distinctive difference between being an expert and being an authority. As one might suspect, an expert is a person who is very skillful or highly trained and informed in some special field. Writers who become increasingly proficient in achieving publication, for example, doubly fulfill the meaning of the word. They may become perceived as experts in the field or subject about which they write, and they may become experts at being published.

Being recognized as an authority requires expertise and a little more. It requires that others rely on an opinion as the definitive statement about a specific matter. Along with recognized authority comes power derived from the respect and esteem of others. Authors of authoritative statements often are given the right to lead by recognized experts based on a record of reliability in a specialized area. The evidence of record frequently consists of quality published materials extending over many years.

The point of mentioning authorities and experts is not to commence a philosophical treatise about power or rights but to dramatize the impact derived from publishing. For the purpose of this book, a single published article indeed can affect its author's life and career depending on how it is received by those who read it and how its author responds to notoriety.

Command Performances

After a writer becomes a published author, what is left to do but repeat the process? Certainly that is what generally follows, although many other options become available. Chapter 9, for example, mentioned service on editorial boards of professional journals as a possibility. As a known published author, invitations sometimes begin finding their way to you requesting services as an editor or reviewer. Such requests may come from your workplace or from an organization of which you are a member, your church or local civic group, from virtually anywhere that others perceive a need for printed communication. Remember, you may be the only person in their midst who has published. You are indeed someone special in that regard in their estimation.

Published authors also begin receiving requests for public speaking engagements because they are seen by others as having something worthwhile to say. You are becoming an expert. As your list of writing and publications grows, it may seem to be easier to have your manuscripts published. Your success may be partially related to the writing practice acquired with each new endeavor. It may also be that reviewers are beginning to recognize (and more readily accept) your writing style. Soon you notice other authors are citing your works. You are on the fringes of becoming a recognized authority. More invitations to speak. More invitations to write. More requests to participate in groups. More requests to serve your profession and its constituency. More opportunities for expenses-paid travel. More.

Could this happen to you after reading this book? Maybe. The point is that it happens to some writers. While such demands may be food for a hungry ego at first, a point of satiation approaches and with it the appetite for recognition and the fun of writing can burn out. To avoid such a plight, pacing and judgment are necessary. Recognize the limits of your endurance and the effects of these demands on your family, work, and leisure activities. Learn to politely refuse more invitations than you are willing to devote time to completing or are capable of juggling with other responsibilities. Writing and its rewards can become enjoyable and fulfilling as long as you remember to organize and pace yourself.

Conclusion

The purpose of this book has been to provide concise, comprehensive, and practical information focusing on proven methods that enhance manuscript publication. We hope the contents will serve as an aid to those who are beginning professional writing activities, as well as those with experience who wish to learn about new dissemination sources, or who truly desire to overcome some block concerning certain methods or techniques.

This book is based on our experiences in getting published and on the research of many other experts and authorities. *Persist and Publish* has examined and discussed the entire range of academic writing and publishing. Formulated from years of teaching academic writing and providing faculty development activities at diverse and distant universities, the end result has been to lead new or inexperienced academicians through the exciting venture that is or will become an integral part of their careers.

More often than not writing this book was an enjoyable experience, though at times it was tedious. We hope that neither evidence of the latter was readily apparent, nor that the process of reading it proved the same. Should our effort result in one reader achieving a single publication who otherwise would not have tried, the purpose of *Persist and Publish* will have been achieved.

Annotated Bibliography

Aleamoni, L. M., and M. Yimer. 1973. An investigation of the relationship between colleague rating, student rating, research productivity, and academic rank in rating instructional effectiveness. *Journal of Educational Psychology* 64(3): 274–77.

A total of 477 University of Illinois faculty were studied in the fall of 1969–70. The examination found that academic publications are more highly related to academic rank than to peer or student ratings or gender.

Alley, B., and J. Cargill. 1986. *Librarian in search of a publisher: How to get published.* Phoenix, Ariz.: Oryx.

A specialized text which examines, from a how-to perspective, academic publishing for college and university librarians. Although many sections are based wholly on library materials many chapters are generic and provide excellent information for any publishing scholar.

Appelbaum, J., and N. Evans. 1978. *How to get happily published.* New York: Harper & Row.

Important facts: (1) Publishers need you, need good material, and need fresh talent. (2) Editors make errors. Many books which were rejected went on to make publishing history. (3) There should be an editor somewhere who is looking for what you have to offer — perseverance pays.

Atkinson, D. R., M. J. Furlong, and B. E. Wampold. 1982. Statistical significance, reviewer evaluations, and the scientific process: Is there a (statistically) significant relationship? *Journal of Counseling Psychology* 29(2): 189–94.

An empirical study which found that manuscripts that detailed statistical significance were three times more likely to be published than reports of studies which were nonsignificant statistically. A total of fifty APA consulting editors were queried.

Bailey, H. S., Jr. 1988. The future of university press publishing. *Scholarly Publishing* 19(2): 63–69.

A senior statesman of scholarly publishing examines the future of university presses. The miniboom, the need for teachers, and disillusionment with the yuppie life-style and with the MBA as the key to a career lead to an increased use of universities and their presses. Finds that the fate of university presses will rise or fall with the fate of scholarship and higher education.

Baker, S. S. 1982. Writing proposals that get book contracts. *The Writer* 95(3): 7–11.

Contract-getting suggestions by an author of over twenty-five books. Provide facts only and eliminate all extraneous material from proposal; the editor is seeking a profit-making book.

Bali, M. 1984. A writer's guide to buying a word processor. *The Writer* 97(4): 5–8.

Detailed information about selecting a microcomputer word processor. Lists requirements for the program, computer, storage, printer, and monitor.

Bayer, A. E., and J. E. Dutton. 1977. Career age and research-professional activities of academic scientists. *Journal of Higher Education* 48(3): 259–82.

Based on a 1972–73 national study of 5,079 Ph.D.-level teaching faculty in 259 colleges and universities. Prime investigation variable was career age. Found that the number of published articles in the last two years was 1–2 articles (28.8 percent); 5+ articles by 27.4 percent of faculty. Total number of published articles: 3–10 (31.2 percent), 11–20 (21.1 percent), and 21+ total articles by 32 percent of faculty. Total number of books and monographs: 1–2 (30.5 percent), 5+ books by 9.6 percent of faculty.

Bean, J. C. 1983. Computerized word-processing as an aid to revision. *College Composition and Communication* 34(2): 146–48.

A study which found that beginning writers learn to revise initial drafts with more emphasis on shaping and focusing stages using a word processor. Eliminated concern for rewrites by providing current, freshly typed scripts.

Bodian, N. G. 1988. *How to choose a winning title: A guide for writers, editors, and publishers.* Phoenix, Ariz.: Oryx.

Provides a practical guide to book and article titling. Examines legal aspects, origins of best-selling titles, the publisher's perspective, marketing aspects, psychological aspects, and notable failures.

Boice, R. 1987a. *Psychological approaches to facilitating writing.* Long Beach: California State University. (Unpublished paper available from the Center for Faculty Development.)

A brief outline of the salient characteristics of writing that can be discussed between academic mentors and protégés. Included in the outline are the identified psychological elements and their relational functions with various aspects of the academic writing process.

————. 1987b. *Writing problems.* Long Beach: California State University. (Unpublished paper available from the Center for Faculty Development.)

A substantial review of psychological and related approaches to writing problems. The paper provides a historical overview of interest in the topic, followed by a comprehensive summary of the literature concerning writing problems. The paper concludes with three considerations: evidence supporting the effectiveness of diagnosing and treating the problem; a hierarchical ranking of the sources of writing problems; and traditional controversies that inhibit the study of writing as an understandable and treatable problem.

Boice, R., and K. Johnson. 1984. Perception and practice of writing for publication by faculty at a doctoral-granting university. *Research in Higher Education* 21(1): 33–43.

Four hundred faculty members at SUNY-Albany (58 percent return rate) responded concerning their perception and practice of academic publishing. Excellent discussion of productivity and faculty development.

Bridgwater, C.A., P. H. Bornstein, and J. Walkenbach. 1981. Ethical issues and the assignment of publication credit. *American Psychologist* 36(5): 524–25.

A total of 261 academic psychologists (27.5 percent return rate) from forty doctoral-level programs were queried. Found that contribution and subsequent publication credit depended on scholarly importance of work, not time, energy, status, pay, or supervision.

Budd, J. 1982. Book reviewing practices of journals in the humanities. *Scholarly Publishing* 13(4): 363–71.

Fifty-eight journal editors (89.2 percent) responded to a survey concerning book review practices. The journals reviewed an average of fifty-six books per year, with a publication lag of seven months. Thirty-two of the editors (55.2 percent) stated that they do not accept unsolicited book reviews for publication.

Buddemeier, R. W. 1981. Least publishable unit. *Science* 212(4494): 494.

Notes problems and concerns involved with journals publishing fragmented, or portions of, completed studies: (1) incentive to get publication mileage out of interim and final reports, (2) increase in specialization of journals, (3) funding tied to research record, and (4) multiple authorships.

Cappeto, M. A., and W. E. Kauffman. 1983. Steps to professional writing. *Journal of College Placement* 43(3) : 33–36.

Eight steps to professional writing are examined: Why you want to be published, determining your audience, selecting the medium, reading targeted medium, listing of topics, making two outlines, selecting one and writing, and reading aloud.

Caute, D., and G. Graham. 1983. Contacts and contracts. *The Times Higher Education Supplement* (December 2): 14–15.

Clearly examines the intent of book publishing contracts which frequently contain at least twenty clauses. Details what the publisher requires of authors and what the publisher commits to: copyright, manuscript deliverance, illustrations, index, proofing, advance payment, royalties, subsidiary rights, and complimentary copies.

Centra, J. A. 1983. Research productivity and teaching effectiveness. *Research in Higher Education* 18(2): 379–89.

Extensive dual research studies that examine the research-teaching relationship. Surveyed 2,973 faculty members from sixty-one four-year low emphasis on research institutions and 1,623 faculty at ten institutions with more emphasis on research productivity. Found 1.7 publications during a five-year period (49 percent no publications) in the first sample, and 2.5 publications (44 percent none) in the second sample. Overall found little support for link between research and teaching performance; however, a modest relationship was found in social sciences.

Clemente, F. 1973. Early career determinants of research productivity. *American Journal of Sociology* 79(2): 409–19.

A total of 2,205 Ph.D.s who were members of the American Sociological Association in 1970 were surveyed. Found that early publication activity indicated enhanced subsequent productivity. Gender, rate of educational progress, and Ph.D. training department had less impact on academic publications.

Cole, S., and J. R. Cole. 1967. Scientific output and recognition: A study in the operation of the reward system in science. *American Sociological Review* 32(3): 377–90.

Sampled 120 university physicists drawn from an effective survey of 1,281 (65.5 percent return). Found quality of publications more important to recognition (awards, appointments, visibility) than quantity of articles.

Conciatore, J. 1990. Trying to publish, not perish: Black scholars may find obstacles. *Black Issues in Higher Education* 7(9): 1, 3–4.

Many blacks lack access to publishers through the informal network of peers. Additionally few professors may relate to some students what is required in the publishing arena. With only 4 percent of all full-time college and university faculty members being black, minority students will often need to find a white professor for a mentor.

Cox, W. M., and J. P. Blount. 1989. Research and productivity in psychology. (Comment). *American Psychologist* 44(4): 735–36.

In examining previous research, the authors find that a psychology department that has a mixture of frequent and not so frequent publishers — some who are interested in teaching and advising — may be a better department than one exclusively filled with highly productive faculty from a publishing point of view.

Day, R. A. 1988. *How to write and publish a scientific paper.* Phoenix, Ariz.: Oryx.

A superb how-to cookbook providing technical information about scientific publications. Particularly eloquent concerning English usage. Chapters on: preparing the title, listing authors and addresses, abstracting the paper, introducing the project, developing materials and methods sections, structuring results, developing an appropriate discussion, stating the acknowledgments, citing references, designing effective tables and illustrations, and keyboarding the manuscript.

Denham, A. 1982. Publishing in education journals: Practical advice for contributors. *Texas Tech Journal of Education* 9(3): 203–14.

Answers the basic questions of prospective journal contributors on getting started, selecting a journal, and increasing the likelihood of getting an article accepted.

Denham, A., and W. Broom. 1981. The role of the author. *Scholarly Publishing* 12(3): 249–58.

A discussion of what professional editors, of both journals and books, require of authors. The obligation to be active and involved in the publishing process belongs to the author who must understand the editorial and production processes.

Dillon, J. T. 1981. The emergence of the colon: An empirical correlate of scholarship. *American Psychologist* 36(8): 879–84.

In order to increase the probability of publications in a scholarly journal the author suggests using a colon and between fifteen to twenty words in the title (72 percent of cases inspected). In addition the title preferably should be dysrhythmic in style.

Dorn, F. J. 1980. Book reviewing: The counselor's first step in publication. *The School Counselor* 27(5): 408–9.

Explores how to obtain texts from book companies for review. Simply write to a book publisher, tell them you wish to do an unsolicited review, and request a specific book. In the review: grab attention, be informative, don't personalize, and provide substance in a short and concise review.

———. 1985a. *Publishing for professional development.* Muncie, Ind.: Accelerated Development Inc.

A how-to book for the novice professional writer. Devotes chapters to a wide range of topics: reasons for writing, generating ideas, time management, marketing, the evaluation process, experimental, review, and theoretical articles, and books. Chapters are also devoted to topics rarely examined: query letters, coping with rejection, book reviewing, writing for state journals, "in the field" articles, and free-lance opportunities.

———. 1985b. Developing your publication potential and copyright confidence. *Journal of Counseling and Development* 63(8): 512–14.

A discussion of the developmental process in writing counseling articles. In brief consider the following points: have a fresh perspective on the issue, write as you speak, do not send the first draft, examine published manuscript guidelines, expect a request for revision, and identify at least five periodicals appropriate for your manuscript.

Dougherty, A. M. 1982. The publishing counselor. *School Counselor* 30(2): 133–37.

Details four helpful areas for counselors wishing to get into print. Philosophical resignation: be realistic, avoid egoism, defer gratification, confidence, and desire. Prewriting activities: examine journals, work with a professional, involve others, style, typing, query letters. Writing: revise, devil's advocate, tape draft, references. After submission: persistence and negotiation.

Eichorn, D. H., and G. R. VandenBos. 1985. Dissemination of scientific and professional knowledge. *American Psychologist* 40(12): 1309–16.

An excellent article on how to publish for the American Psychological Association. For the novice writer, a step-by-step review of the editorial process is provided.

Figgins, M. A., and H. J. Burbach. 1989. Preparing our students to publish: Lessons learned. *Innovation in Higher Education* 14(1): 15–23.

Details the graduate seminar on writing for professional publication at the University of Virginia's Curry School of Education. Emphasizes collegial writing — professors and students working as colleagues — through a nontraditional course mode, employing cooperative learning and drawing on schoolwide faculty to broaden perspectives.

Fine, T. 1987. Program profile: Getting into print — A guide to research publications. *Psychiatric Research Report* 2(3): 8–9.

This issue of the published newsletter of the American Psychiatric Association Office of Research provides an excellent summary of the format requirements of fifteen noted periodicals in the field of psychiatry. The author provides suggestions about writing that are applicable for each of the journals mentioned.

Flory, M. B. 1983. Semantics and symbioses: How to write an article to impress your peers. *The Chronicle of Higher Education* (January 26): 72.

A tongue-in-cheek approach to article writing that suggests "it is central to success to make it as difficult to read as possible as soon as possible."

Forman, B. D. 1988. Writing for publication. *Counselor Education and Supervision* 28(2): 181–85.

Describes twenty-one stages in writing for publication: developing an idea, choosing individual versus collaborative authorship, organizing the ideas, preparing the first draft, fantasizing abandonment, completing the first draft, soliciting comments, rewriting, soliciting comments again, completing the final draft, submitting the manuscript, waiting, coping with reviewer's comments, resubmitting, receiving the acceptance letter, surviving the publication lag, proofreading, obtaining reprints, seeing your work in print, responding to requests for reprints, and looking for citations.

Fox, M. F., and C. A. Faver. 1982. The process of collaboration in scholarly research. *Scholarly Publishing* 13(4): 327–39.

Examines the growth of collaboration due to organizational, institutional and individual factors, via a nonrandom sample, through semistructured, in-depth interviews of twenty social scientists. Choice of collaborative partners due to intellectual and personal factors.

Task-relationship-structural variables include: rank, gender, number, sharing, skill, time, resources, control, schedules, and contracts.

Frantz, T. T. 1968. Criteria for publishable manuscripts. *Personnel and Guidance Journal* 47(4): 384–86.

Sixty questionnaires (76 percent response rate) were returned by members of the editorial boards of six journals. Criteria for evaluation of manuscripts ranked in importance: contribution to knowledge, design of study, objectivity in reporting results, topic selection, writing style and readability, practical implications, statistical analyses, theoretical model, and review of literature.

Friedrich, R. J., and S. J. Michalak, Jr. 1983. Why doesn't research improve teaching? *Journal of Higher Education* 54(2): 145–63.

Seventy-four faculty at Franklin and Marshall College were studied to determine relationship between research and teaching. The complex study found that research accounts for only 2.89 percent of the variation in teaching effectiveness, a correlation of only 0.17.

Fulton, O., and M. Trow. 1974. Research activity in American higher education. *Sociology of Education* 47(1): 29–73.

Reports on the 1969 Carnegie Survey of 60,028 faculty (60 percent return) in 300 colleges and universities. Found 24 percent had a very heavy interest in research. A total of 48 percent reported current publications. Concerning hours in class 37 percent reported 6 to 0 hours per week. Full professors reported highest level of research activity.

Funk, R. W. 1977. Issues in scholarly publishing. *Scholarly Publishing* 9(1): 3–17.

A critique of an extensive study. The study cited failed to appropriately account for the learned society and the university itself in the scheme of production and dissemination of scholarly knowledge.

Gay, J. T., and A. E. Edgil. 1989. When your manuscript is rejected. *Nursing & Health Care* 10(8): 459–61.

Breaks down examination of rejected manuscripts into factors related to design, content, and writing style. Found many rejections stemmed from inadequate preparation prior to developing the manuscript.

Germano, W. P. 1983. Helping the local faculty with publication support. *Scholarly Publishing* 15(1): 11–16.

A survey of 110 departments of English and to a lesser degree romance languages in state and private institutions of higher learning. The purpose of the study was to determine if presses, projects, or authors were receiving publication subsidies to assist in developing books. The results were not untypical, as private institutions had more monies to distribute for the purpose. However, over half of the respondents stated some kind of subsidy program was in operation.

Gladding, S. T. 1984. Multiple authorship in the Personnel and Guidance Journal: A 12-year study. *Personnel and Guidance Journal* 62(10): 628–30.

With an acceptance rate of about 25 percent the journal examined authorship for a twelve-year period 1971–82. Found a trend that indicated fewer single-authored articles were being published. Possible reasons discussed: pressure to publish for tenure, more collaboration, more special issues, emphasis on networking, and mentoring.

Glenn, N. D. 1976. The journal article review process: Some proposals for change. *The American Sociologist* 11(3): 179–85.

Journals disseminate findings, provide a gatekeeper function, and confer recognition and rewards. To continue these functions with too many manuscripts being submitted and limited human resources being available, changes in the manuscript review process should be made: (1) Editors should reject highly improbable manuscripts immediately. (2) Editorial decisions and selecting referees should be spread over three to four professionals. (3) Reviewers should provide written feedback. (4) All papers should be sent to at least three reviewers.

Goodwin, L. R., Jr. 1988. The rehabilitation counselor education job search: A practical guide for the applicant. *Journal of Applied Rehabilitation Counseling* 19(1): 37–42.

Provides a job search checklist for rehabilitation counselor educators. Examines course options, teaching load, summer school teaching, financial aspects, and tenure. Notes that publications expectations are: high = 2 or more refereed journal articles per year, moderate = 1 or less, low = 1 or 2 publications for tenure over a five- to seven-year period.

Graburn, N.H.H. 1981. University press books in the classroom. *Scholarly Publishing* 13(1): 70–78.

Considers the problem of academic books being published for expected large-volume sales rather than for quality and the dissemination of knowledge.

Grannis, C. B. 1988. Book title output and average prices: 1987 preliminary figures. In F. Simora, M. Spier, and D. Gray, eds. *The Bowker Annual of Library and Book Trade.* 33rd ed. New York: R. R. Bowker Co.

Accounts that the total 1987 title production numbering 45,401 in the preliminary computation, may well be close to the 52,637 counted for all of 1986. Rough estimates find close to 52,000 titles a year, made up of 32,000 hardcover books, 16,000 non-mass market paperback, and 4,000 mass market titles. Average price of hardcover books is $35.35, up 8 percent over the 1986 final figure of $32.43.

Greaser, C. U. 1979. Improving the effectiveness of research writing. *Scholarly Publishing* 11(1): 61–71.

Details an experimental effective writing workshop at the Rand Corporation. The corporation has a 500-member research staff and has found that university training generally neglects professional writing.

Haney, D. Q. 1988. Does anybody read this stuff? *Southern Illinoisan* (July 31): 25.

In 1665 *Le Journal des Savants* was first published in Paris. At the start of the eighteenth century, there were 100 journals. By the beginning of the twentieth century, there were 10,000. Currently there are somewhere between 40,000 to 60,000 journals in publication. Author queries if anyone has the time to read all these journals, even the professionals for whom they are intended.

Hanna, S. S. 1983. Looking for a publisher. *Publishers Weekly* 224(20): 17–19.

The author examines the eight different categories/formats of rejections he received trying to obtain a book contract. He is still looking for a publisher.

Henson, K. T. 1984. Writing for professional publication: Ways to increase your success. *Phi Delta Kappan* 65(8): 635–37.

Author queried forty-one education journals about a number of characteristics which are well illustrated in a table: acceptance rate, length, refereed, percentage research, articles per year, issues per year, university personnel contributors, query letters, days to answer, receipt time, weeks to decision, and effect of photos. Interesting data include: four fifths of manuscripts rejected, three fourths of contributors university personnel, two thirds of editors do not want query letters, most frequent mistake is failing to acquaint with journal, readers, and submission guidelines.

—————. 1988. Writing for education journals. *Phi Delta Kappan* 69(10): 752–54.

Of a total of forty-nine education journal editors (response rate of 75 percent) 44 percent said their journals were not refereed. Average rejection rate was 72 percent. Response time to query letters is twelve days, manuscript acknowledgment is an average of eleven days, publication decision average is eleven weeks. Nineteen percent of editors do not want query letters or phone calls.

Hickson, M., III, D. W. Stacks, and J. H. Amsbary. 1989. An analysis of prolific scholarship in speech communication, 1915–1985. Toward a yardstick for measuring research productivity. *Communication Education* 38(3): 230–36.

Examined speech communication literature over a seventy-year period. Found that most of the prolific authors had published within one year prior to receiving a doctoral degree or within three years after; data support importance of publishing early in one's career. Found research habits begin early and research breeds more research.

Hogan, J. C., and S. Cohen. 1965. *An author's guide to scholarly publishing and the law.* Englewood Cliffs, N.J.: Prentice-Hall.

Surveys the steps in finding a publisher for a book: (1) Consult *The Literary Marketplace,* a directory of the book-publishing trade. (2) Survey other books in the field to find a range of publishers. (3) Do not look for a literary agent for your scholarly book. (4) Write to the main office of the publisher. (5) Submit an appropriate prospectus. (6) Send prospectus to a dozen or so publishers at the same time. (7) Revise dissertations — some publishers will not examine them until this has been done.

Hoge, J. O., and J.L.W. West III. 1979. Academic book reviewing: Some problems and suggestions. *Scholarly Publishing* 11(1): 35–41.

The low status given to published book reviews caused by: lack of editorial attention, lax standards, mediocre reviews, reviewers not carefully selected, little scrutiny, time lags, and reviews not taken seriously for promotion and tenure considerations. Offers suggestions to enhance quality and respectability of book reviews.

Holmes, M. 1982. Formula for success. *The Writer* 95(11): 9–11, 23.

A best-selling author offers several suggestions to new writers: (1) Talent for writing is a gift. (2) Talent can only be developed through study and practice. (3) Failure is when you stop trying. Expect rejection of your work. Expect to rewrite and rewrite your work. And expect to succeed. (4) Write every day.

Hood, A. B. 1984. Knowledge dissemination and the role of professional journals. *Journal of College Student Personnel* 25(1): 17–18.

Notes that the role and function of a journal in an applied field differs from that of a scientific journal. The applied journal, such as *JCSP,* exists primarily for the readers (in this case mostly practitioners), although nearly half of the article authors are university professors. An applied journal relates basic knowledge to the field and reports applied field experimental data.

Hoover, K. H. 1980. Responsibilities for professional growth: Writing techniques. Chap. 17 in *College teaching today*. Boston: Allyn and Bacon, Inc.

Generally examines the approaches and techniques of professional writing. An excellent brief section on the value of such writing: affords visible leadership role, keeps up with latest developments, increases teaching competence, and rewards. Limitations and problems equally examined: some unable to become competent writers, too much a part of professional evaluations, time and effort interfere with other activities, little consideration for quality, and excessive publication time lags.

Hosford, B. 1990. *Winning in your profession by writing books*. Springfield, Ill.: Charles C. Thomas.

A how-to book for professionals in the biomedical and behavioral sciences and the law. Comprehensive examination of book writing and publishing, including an examination of the need for literary agents and how to boost book sales.

Howe, M. R. 1982. Help for the scholar-author. *Scholarly Publishing* 13(2): 157–66.

Carefully reviews the various roles of the free-lance editor. As more publishers are using free-lance editors the scholar-publisher should understand both the publisher-editor and free-lance-editor functions.

Hoyt, D. P. 1974. Interrelationships among instructional effectiveness, publication record, and monetary reward. *Research in Higher Education* 2(1): 81–88.

A correlation study of 222 Kent State University faculty with two or more years found that teacher effectiveness was not related to academic publications. Modest relationship existed with fiscal rewards.

Jalongo, M. R. 1987. On the compatibility of teaching and scholarly writing. *Scholarly Publishing* 18(4): 49–58.

Although often cited as a drain on energies that would be better spent on improving teaching, publishing and teaching are remarkably similar. Notes that the benefits of writing for the teacher include: (1) sphere of influence who they reach, (2) teaching materials — information to support lectures, (3) knowledge of field — deeper level of understanding, and (4) scholarly role fulfillment of needs for belongingness and for esteem.

Johnson, N. 1982. Publishing: How to get started. *Personnel and Guidance Journal* 60(5): 321–22.

Tips on how to overcome fear of failure and lack of confidence finally leading to: overcoming fear of statistics, picking the right outlet, developing and writing an article, submission guidelines, manuscript revision, and patience.

Jones, J. E., G. C. Preusz, and S. N. Finkelstein. 1989. Factors associated with clinical dental faculty research productivity. *Journal of Dental Education* 53(11): 638–45.

Found that past research funding, career age, training status, establishment interaction, and conducting research from planned goals enabled prediction of research productivity. Cited several medical studies which showed two peaks of scientific accomplishment — young faculty (6–11 years) and second peak (18–23 years) — and a decline after thirty years. Collaboration increases productivity.

Katz, S. B., J. T. Kapes, and P. A. Zirkel. 1980. *Resources for writing for publication in education*. New York: Teachers College Press.

A how-to book which specializes in academic publishing in the field of education. An excellent introductory chapter examining the importance of academic publications: monetary rewards, contributions and usefulness, and activities which promote publishing. Chapters on conference and convention papers, journals, books and monographs, indices, manuals and guides, and copyright information.

King, C. M. 1989. Research productivity in the education of hearing impaired individuals. *The Journal of Speech Education* 23(3): 279–93.

Examined 2,541 articles for a six-year period. Found only 22 of 2,747 authors had published six or more empirical articles during the period. Fifty-seven authors had a mean of at least one article of any kind per year. One individual, who had the highest number of articles overall, had ten empirical and ten nonempirical articles published during the six-year period.

Klemp, P. J. 1981. Reviewing academic books: Some ideas for beginners. *Scholarly Publishing* 12(2): 135–39.

Briefly examines what the author sees as the steps in book reviewing. Comments concerning assessing the audience that will read the review, and who the book author saw as an appropriate book user.

Leslie, L. Z. 1989. Manuscript review: A view from below. *Scholarly Publishing* 20(2): 123–28.

Provides personal experiences of a individual trying to get published. Examines and makes recommendations about journal operation and efficiency.

———. 1990. Peer review practices of mass communication scholarly journals. *Education Review* 14(2): 151–65.

Found that only eighteen of the top researchers in mass communication average one full article per year in refereed journals. Reviewers of manuscripts spend on the average 3.44 hours reviewing submissions and that respondents were least satisfied with the time required for an accepted article to be published.

Levitt, B., and C. Nass. 1989. Lid on the garbage can: Institutional constraints on decision making in the technical core of college-text publishers. *Administrative Science Quarterly* 34(2): 190–207.

A study of college physics and sociology textbook publishers. Found that the institutional environment limits the range of problems, solutions, and choice opportunities flowing into the technical core. This factor is a key source of ordering the technical core and its outputs.

Luey, B. 1987. *Handbook for academic authors.* Cambridge: Cambridge University Press.

An excellent text from an experienced author and editor which provides a useful overview of academic writing and publishing. For the more experienced, chapter 10 concerning costs and prices of books is particularly illuminating. Includes other chapters on the publishing partnership, revising a dissertation, working with your publisher, and the mechanics of authorship.

———. 1989. Technology and the author's labour. *Scholarly Publishing* 20(2): 72–83.

Looks to the future of publishing by looking to the past and making comparisons. Notes increasing author involvement in the manufacture of their books.

McConnell, J. V. 1978. Confessions of a textbook writer. *American Psychologist* 33(2): 159–69.

Examines the problem of introductory texts being encyclopedic but also dramatic so that students remember the material. Students prefer a text which is simple, well-organized, coherent, comprehensive yet interesting. Unfortunately instructors find such books too simple.

McGiffert, M. 1988. Is justice blind? An inquiry into peer review. *Scholarly Publishing* 20(1): 43–48.

Brings new light to the age-old question of whether reviews should be blind. Recommends that editors poll their advisory boards.

McKeon, J. J. 1983. Should you try book publishing? *Association Management* 35(7): 77–83.

Examines why and how a professional association (not an individual) can publish a book.

McMillen, L. 1986. A doctoral dissertation is not yet a book, young tenure-seeking scholars are told. *Chronicle of Higher Education* 31(21): 23–24.

Suggested tips for publishing a dissertation: (1) make material interesting, (2) eliminate extensive documentation, (3) write for a specific reader, (4) do research on publishers before submitting.

MacPhail, B. D. 1980. Book reviews and the scholarly publisher. *Scholarly Publishing* 12(1): 55–63.

Outlines advantages of book reviews. For publishers — promotion, evaluation, and very cost effective. For readers — information and ideas for new directions. Publishers feel a 1 to 2 percent response on a promotional mailing (flyers) is good. For 2,000-copy edition, 100 complimentary books may be sent out.

McQuaid, E. P. 1982. Authors of scholarly books urged to set publishing guidelines. *The Chronicle of Higher Education* (June 2): 23.

Details the formation of a national writers union. The union would establish guidelines concerning scholarly manuscript publication and lobby to increase the financing of grants and royalties.

Mager, R. F. 1986. *The how to write a book book.* Carefree, Ariz.: Mager Associates, Inc.

A good overall perspective on writing and publishing books. The book was self-published due to disagreements with the original contract publisher/editor.

Mann, P. H. 1981. Publishing the scholarly author. *Scholarly Publishing* 12(2): 99–108.

Addresses the symbiotic relationship between author and publisher through an analysis of seventy-two academic books published by five British companies. Recommendations include: (1) New scholars should meet publishers early. (2) Authors should understand publishing economics. (3) Authors should understand that time is money and agreements (due dates) should be honored. (4) Publishers have different subject interests. (5) Make contracts simple.

Mansbridge, R. 1980. "My publishers are terrible . . ." *Scholarly Publishing* 11(2): 133–40.

Helps authors to be aware of problems that others have had with their publishers. Examples: Too much editing, poor communication, unfulfilled promises of advertising, serious errors in manufacturing (binding, jackets), and violated contracts.

Markland, M. F. 1983. Taking criticism — and using it. *Scholarly Publishing* 14(2): 139–48.

"Don't ask for criticism unless you really want it" and "Don't try to prove your critic wrong" are the basic principles of receiving criticism. Examines what reviewer comments really mean and suggests action.

Meyer, S., and L. E. Phillabaum. 1980. What is a university press? *Scholarly Publishing* 11(3): 213–19.

A university press serves basically two functions: (1) advancement of knowledge between scholar and scholar, and (2) bridging the gap between the academic community and society at large. The university press distinctly faces the responsibility of serving not only university faculty but functions as part of the book publishing industry and hence nonacademic publishing.

Mills, R. M. 1983. Tradition and innovation in scholarly publishing. *Scholarly Publishing* 15(1): 41–50.

The undue time, length, and cost of the publishing process is examined. The citation system and ways to make easier and earlier recognition of innovative approaches are delineated. Traditional, current methods do not meet the new needs of academic publishing.

Mirman, R. 1975. For open refereeing. *American Journal of Physics* 43(9): 837.

Makes the argument that often reviewers need incentives to do critiques properly, and that criticism appears openly for published papers and should as well for reviews.

Morton, H. C. 1980. Research on the printed word: A review. *Scholarly Publishing* 11(4): 361–70.

A review of a four-volume examination of scholarly publishing. The four volumes, which examine book publishing, journals, libraries, and a summary volume dealing with books, journals, and bibliographic services, were assisted by the National Science Foundation and the National Endowment for the Humanities among others. The series features an economic orientation to academic publishing. In the 1200 plus pages considerable data is provided.

Morton, H. C., A. J. Price, and R. C. Mitchell. 1989. *ACLS survey of scholars: Final report of views on publications, computers, and libraries.* Lanham, Md.: University Press of America.

Response by 3,835 members of ACLS to a fourteen-page survey. Found a rapid increase in the use of computers as compared to past studies, most saw favoritism in peer-review system for journals, and three out of four have published at least one article in a refereed journal.

Mullins, C. J. 1982. Why a word processor? *The Writer* 95(8): 19–22.

Provides the basic facts about types of word processors, i.e., dedicated systems and personal computer programs. The author encourages such an investment because: (1) Quality of typing and setting is professional. (2) Output of work is about four times greater. (3) Processors have memory banks to retrieve names, addresses, and whole manuscripts, and aids revision, and in catching spelling errors. (4) Word processors take from a day to a week to master.

Nelson, R. P. 1978. Book design. Chap. 12 in *Publication design.* 2d ed. Dubuque, Iowa: Wm. C. Brown Co.

An excellent chapter which covers "the look of the book" as well as an overall understanding of book publishing. Several hundred publishers, some doing 600 to 700 titles, put out about 40,000 different books per year.

Noble, K. A. 1989. Publish or perish: What 23 journal editors have to say. *Studies in Higher Education* 14(1): 97–102.

Found a manuscript with a professional appearance appealed to editors. Immediate rejection comes when author guidelines are not followed or manuscript is not thorough or is badly written. Suggest authors write clearly, logically, and sequentially and study and follow the author guidelines.

Oberrecht, K. 1985. Outlines that sell books. *The Writer* 98(5): 19–22.

Reveals that although most book contracts are obtained through an outline and a sample of chapters, outlines alone can do the job. Provides an excellent perspective to developing effective (contract-obtaining) book outlines.

O'Brien, C. R., and J. Johnson. 1980. Promoting professional development skills. *Journal of College Student Personnel* 21(6): 568–69.

Details a workshop approach at Western Illinois University for convention presentations and academic publishing. Publishing segment: determine content, pick appropriate journal, prepare manuscript, and use reviewers' comments.

Ostrowski, P. M., and S. Bartel. 1985. Assisting practitioners to publish through the use of support groups. *Journal of Counseling and Development* 63(8): 510–11.

Focuses its attention toward practitioners in the field who wish to publish. The tool used to facilitate the focus is support groups. Guidelines to general operation are: (1) Formulate goals of the group (writing to promote career development, sharing ideas, continuing education). (2) Have a regular meeting date. (3) Provide motivation to group members. (4) Give immediate feedback to group members.

Parrish, P. S. 1983. Seven ways to lengthen a publication list without doing anything very original. *Chronicle of Higher Education* 26(12): 64.

A not so tongue-in-cheek article based on the assumptions that: a long publication list of any sort is better than a short one, nobody in the department actually reads the material, and abstruse titles are impressive.

Pascal, N. B. 1982. How much editing is enough? *Scholarly Publishing* 13(3): 263–68.

Financial realities (time-cost) often limit considered, dedicated editing. Camera-ready copy and word processing are ways to pass some cost back to the author allowing editing to concentrate on traditional matters (style, values, approach).

Penaskovic, R. 1985. Facing up to the publication gun. *Scholarly Publishing* 16(2): 136–40.

Author covers seven publishing survival skills: (1) Try to overcome lack of motivation — no remuneration for article writing. (2) Know that ideas are everywhere — be attuned to them. (3) Make sure articles have the point clearly stated at the beginning. (4) Don't read too much — start writing. (5) Use a fresh angle — write what no one else has. (6) Try to write in snatches if you don't have large blocks of time. (7) Use returns (rejections) as a means of free criticism.

Reitt, B. B. 1980. The editor turns teacher. *Scholarly Publishing* 11(3): 256–66.

Examines the syllabus of a ten-week graduate-level course at Emory University which is focused toward academic publishing.

———. 1984. An academic author's checklist. *Scholarly Publishing* 16(1): 65–72.

A very detailed checklist to determine the completeness of an article. Major headings include: (1) Is it complete? (2) Is it authoritative? (3) Is it expert? (4) Is it singular? (5) Is it finished? Each of the five headings involves numerous well-formulated questions writers should answer before manuscript submission.

Riggar, T. F., and D. R. Maki. 1980. Stages in professional writing: A guide to authors. *Vocational Evaluation and Work Adjustment Bulletin* 13(1): 9–12.

A description of aspects of technical requirements of professional writing and comments concerning the approaches to developing manuscripts in general. Manuscript development, stylistic format, and the editorial process are presented with considerable clarity. The manuscript development section suggests approaches and factors determining what a budding author should examine.

―――. 1981. An empirical examination of professional publication. *Vocational Evaluation and Work Adjustment Bulletin* 14(1): 32–35.

Found that 90.4 percent of association members were nonuniversity-based personnel. Fifty-two percent of university-based members indicated they had submitted a manuscript to any professional journal, while only 14.5 percent of nonuniversity personnel had ever submitted to any. "No time" was the reason cited by 25 percent of nonuniversity people and by 46 percent of university-based people for not submitting articles for publication. "Don't really care about writing articles in professional journals" was 23 percent for nonuniversity and 8 percent for university-based personnel.

Riggar, T. F., and R. E. Matkin. 1990. Breaking into academic print. *Scholarly Publishing* 22(1): 17–22.

Notes that getting published helps establish credibility in a chosen profession and provides suggestions about how to start. Suggests doing book reviews, refereeing, commentaries, and responding to calls for manuscripts.

Riggs, R. C. 1978. Sources of journal articles in select APGA journals according to academic rank of authors. *Personnel and Guidance Journal* 57(1): 40–41.

Determined academic rank of authors of 492 articles in four American Association of Counseling and Development journals from 1975 to 1977. Overall 41.2 percent of authors indicated no rank, and 52.8 percent reported assistant professor (19 percent), associate professor (17.11 percent), or professor (16.72 percent) rank.

Robinson, P. W., and K. L. Higbee. 1978. Publishing a textbook: Advice from authors and publishers. *Teaching of Psychology* 5(4): 175–81.

A study which queried 108 authors and 16 editors about their publishing experience. Of nearly 3,000 reported manuscripts, 5 percent (154) received contracts. Editors characterized good author attributes as professional activity and academic background (43 percent) and writing experience (23 percent). Most common author problems, 15 percent unwilling to accept reviewer comments.

Rodgers, R. C., and C. L. Maranto. 1989. Causal models of publishing productivity in psychology. *Journal of Applied Psychology* 74(4): 636–49.

Found that high-ability professionals publish more regardless of school attended. Early productivity, quality of first job, and gender of researcher also have impact.

Rodman, H. 1970. The moral responsibility of journal editors and referees. *American Sociologist* 5(4): 351–57.

Queries the often inordinate time it takes to review manuscripts and the size of a journal's backlog (publication delay). Recommends a "contract" between journal editor and reviewers limiting number of reviews and return time limits.

―――. 1978. Some practical advice for journal contributors. *Scholarly Publishing* 9(3): 233–41.

Answers common and practical questions about article publishing. Specifically answers chances for acceptance, selecting a journal, response time, and dealing with rejection.

Rosenfeld, R. R., and J. A. Jones. 1986. Institutional mobility among academics: The case of psychologists. *Sociology of Education* 59(4): 212–26.

Samples the career history of academic psychologists in relation to gender and extent, pattern, and consequences of job mobility. Found mobility led to horizontal moves or moves out of academia. Women gained less from moves, moved more frequently, and moved out of academia quicker.

Roskies, E. 1975. Publish and perish. *American Psychologist* 30(12): 1165–68.

Recounts the seven-plus-year path of getting the author's book published. Notes that not all publications are created equal — senior faculty often possess reputations, staff, and tricks of the trade.

Sachs, H. L. 1988. The publication requirement should not be based solely on "refereed" journals. *The Chronicle of Higher Education* (October 2): B2.

Notes that a university serves many communities besides its own and that journals, particularly academic ones, are read by few people outside the academic community. A university must reach multiple audiences (e.g., recruit students, raise funds), and sometimes nonrefereed journals and magazines get the message across better for the good of the university.

Sattelmeyer, R. 1989. Seven steps to a better review process. *Scholarly Publishing* 20(3): 173–77.

Provides potential solutions to the problem of unreasonable and unconscionable delays in reviews. Makes some interesting points concerning the depth of harm or injury that might befall scholars. A number of all too frequent delays are illustrated.

Seligman, L., and S. C. Kelly. 1990. Writing and publishing books in counseling: A survey of authors. *Journal of Counseling and Development* 69(1): 42–45.

A survey of seventy-four book authors found that they had done 237 books with forty publishers. Thirty-nine percent of books with one coauthor, 11 percent with two coauthors. Fifty-four percent submitted book manuscript to one publisher while 11 percent submitted to eight or more publishers.

Showalter, D. E. 1978. Publication and stagnation in the Liberal Arts College. *Educational Record* 59: 166–72.

Details the differences between the "publish or perish" university and liberal arts colleges. Characterizes faculty who are researchers and avowed cosmopolitans versus the teaching and institutional activity of "locals."

Sikula, J. P. 1979. Writing for publication. *Educational Horizons* 58(2): 97–104.

A synthesized presentation of the various components of writing and publishing that are important for academic faculty in their careers. The manuscript focuses its content on two fundamental aspects of writing: developing the habit of writing through practice and practical steps comprising the mechanics of writing.

Silverman, R. J. 1984. Publishing patterns evidenced in the core higher education journals. *Research in Higher Education* 21(2): 159–77.

Eight core higher education journals from 1975 to 1981 contained 1,103 articles which were examined. Found that 40 percent of first authors on articles were from research universities and that only 1.5 percent of total senior authors were graduate students.

Smith, B. M., and P. B. Gough. 1984. Editors speak out on refereeing. *Phi Delta Kappan* 65(8): 637–39.

Queried editors of 138 refereed and 38 nonrefereed journals. This excellent and detailed study of a number of differences between refereed and nonrefereed found the only real disparity had to do with the range of material published by journal type. Refereed journals are conservative, mainstream, and tend to be negative toward the unusual or controversial. Another important difference is that promotion and tenure committees give higher status to refereed journals.

Smith, J. 1988. Wordsmiths who suffer bad spells. *Los Angeles Times* (April 11), section 5, page 1.

Numerous examples from a newspaper columnist who finds that it is possible to make 10,000 mistakes on one page of a newspaper. Readers provided clips which revealed a wide variety of amusing errors in spelling, grammar, and syntax.

Smith, J. H. 1977. Subvention of scholarly publishing. *Scholarly Publishing* 9(1): 19–29.

Noted a 22 percent reduction of hardback books published by sixty-one university presses (1970–76) because of budgetary problems. Examined parameters of press and institutional policies and practices. Potential solutions offered.

Sorcinelli, M. D. 1985. Profile: The Indiana U Faculty. *Administrator* 4(22): 1–2.

A survey of 112 faculty at Indiana University revealed that not having enough time and time allocation were problems. Teaching and services activities drained time needed for research (time for research primary concern, teaching a secondary concern).

Strahan, R. F. 1982. More on JCP publication: Single versus multiple authorship. *Journal of Counseling Psychology* 29(4): 430–31.

From 1954 to 1979 found an increase from 52.4 percent to 76.7 percent of incidences of multiple authorship in *JCP*. Examines a variety of reasons for the rise of multiple authorship: pressure to publish, sharing the work (two articles better than one), increasing size of academic departments, tendency toward multidisciplinary and interinstitutional work, and editorial policies.

Sugar, J., and C. R. Tracy. 1989. Is the sex of a dissertation advisor related to a young scientist's rate of publication? (Comment). *American Psychologist* 44(3): 574–75.

Noted that there is no evidence that the gender of the advisor has a significant effect on student's publication following graduation. Found that without a more controlled data set cannot assume gender is a causative factor for productivity.

Suppa, R.J., and P. A. Zirkel. 1983. The importance of refereed publications: A national survey. *Phi Delta Kappan* 64(10): 739–40.

A national survey of the institutional representatives of the American Association of Colleges for Teacher Education was conducted in order to determine the importance refereed publications have on promotion and tenure. The majority surveyed were chairpersons or deans of higher education. A 68 percent (494) return concluded that refereed journals were important to promotion and tenure but other factors such as the range of the journals' audience, scholarly presentations, and overall reputation were important issues.

Surwillo, W. W. 1986. Anonymous reviewing and the peer-review process. *American Psychologist* 41(2): 218.

Given that blind reviews where the reviewer knows the name of the author but the author does not know the name of the reviewer, or where neither author nor reviewer is aware of the other's identity have problems, a third alternative is proposed — reviewers know who wrote the manuscript and the author is informed who is doing the review.

Sutherland, J. 1990. The making of codices and careers. *Scholarly Publishing* 21(2): 85–91.

Examines the role of gatekeeper by English-language university presses. Notes that quite unwilling university publishers have become referees as to who can publish in a field and who cannot. Suggests that presses divest themselves of some of the more commercial and authorial functions.

Thompson, R. W. 1987a. Some tentative conclusions about service. Long Beach: California State University. (Unpublished handout available from the Center for Faculty Development.)

A brief summary of ratings about the perceived importance of community and school service in promotion and tenure decisions. Participant responses were made by voluntary members who were assigned mentor or protégé roles as part of a federal grant. Public funding was paid to study the outcomes of mentors assigned to protégés in terms of faculty esprit d'corps, job satisfaction, rate and timeliness of receiving promotion and tenure, and other outcomes of important issues for faculty employed in public institutions of higher education.

―――――. 1987b. Summary of data from the survey on service. Long Beach: California State University. (Unpublished handout available from the Center for Faculty Development.)

Noninterpretive summary of categorical responses of participants that were assigned mentor or protégé roles in a federally funded project concerning higher education employment. Results are presented in statistical and narrative forms.

Tryon, G. S. 1981. Publication records of women counselors during the past decade. *Journal of Counseling Psychology* 28(2): 184–86.

Examines the publication history of women in *JCP* for ten years (1969–79). In 1969 women were 11 percent of authors; by 1979 women authors had increased to 27 percent.

―――――. 1986. Getting published: A personal account. *Journal of Counseling and Development* 64(10): 650.

Recounts the path of the author's 31 published articles in 8 years. Nineteen rejected by first journal submitted to, 3 accepted without revision, 9 revised and resubmitted to the same journal. The median from initial submission to publication was 15 months. Found that patience and persistence are rewarded.

Van Til, W. 1986. *Writing for professional publication.* 2d ed. Boston: Allyn and Bacon.

An excellent book covering the wide range of topics involved in academic writing and publishing. Written as a narrative between an author and an editor, the book offers numerous examples of letters and forms. The twenty-nine chapters cover all relevant topics concerning publishing opportunities, the writer at work, editorial offices, and a miscellany of questions and answers.

Voeks, V. W. 1962. Publication and teaching effectiveness. *Journal of Higher Education* 33(4): 212–18.

A study to determine if there exists a relationship between quality of teaching and research. Faculty members (n = 305) were drawn from thirty departments. Results show that quality of teaching and quality of publishing are independent variables.

Walker, D. A. 1987. Management of scholarly publications. *Scholarly Publishing* 18(3): 189–96.

A response rate of 12.5 percent (182 usable replies) found: (1) The average number of associate editors is fourteen. (2) Nearly half have fewer than eight associate editors (the median value). (3) Sixty-four percent of the journals obtained two reviews per manuscript, and 25 percent obtained three or more reviews. (4) More than 50 percent of the journals received fewer than 100 papers annually. (5) Two thirds of the journals accepted without revision less than 10 percent of the papers they published. (6) The lag time for publication of a paper after it has been accepted is twenty-six weeks or more for 43 percent of the journals.

Walker, J. R. 1978. Writing avoidance: A professional approach. *Personnel and Guidance Journal* 57(4): 218–19.

A six-step system to begin academic writing: (1) developing preliminary mental imagery, (2) conferring/corresponding, (3) planning, (4) covering yourself/anticipating, (5) writing, and (6) resisting pressure.

Walton, J. M. 1982. Research activity and scholarly productivity among counselor educators. *Counselor Education and Supervision* 21(4): 305–11.

A total of 255 counselor educators (56.1 percent return) found 83 high producers (3 or more articles in the last 2 years and 11+ total, or principal investigator, or 3+ monographs or books). Low producers, 172, did not meet criteria. More high producers were tenured (79.5 percent) and over 45 years of age (53.1 percent). All indicated time, insufficient reward, and poor funding as primary factors preventing scholarly publications.

Ward, J. W. 1984. How scholars regard university presses. *Scholarly Publishing* 16(1): 33–38.

Survey results of twenty-two (50 percent return) American Council of Learned Societies delegates concerning how scholars regard university presses. All hold university presses in high regard but express concerns about: pricing policies, publishing high-market value books to buy opportunity to publish others with low-market value, and finding economic alternatives.

Watkins, C. E., Jr. 1982. Writing for publication: Some helpful tips for the school counselor. *School Counselor* 29(3): 239–42.

With journal rejection rates as high as 85 to 90 percent, the author suggests following "journal etiquette." The writer should follow guidelines and be relevant, novel, interested in feedback, concise, careful, neat, patient, and willing to revise.

Weaver, F. S. 1982. Teaching, writing, and developing. *Journal of Higher Education* 53(5): 587–92.

The central issue revolves around better college teaching. Writing can develop better clarity of teaching methods, heighten self-respect, increase visibility of the institution, and strengthen faculty morale by engaging in scholarly issues.

Winkler, K. J. 1984. Scholarly publisher worries about "confusion in the industry." *The Chronicle of Higher Education* (November 28): 11–12.

New ways to cut costs, the fast production of knowledge, defense of shrinking markets, and maintaining the quality of scholarship are causing confusion in the publishing industry. Emphasizing speed, doing books in-house, standardizing formats, authors providing camera-ready copy, less editing, and short press runs are possible solutions.

Winston, R. B., Jr. 1985. A suggested procedure for determining order of authorship in research publications. *Journal of Counseling and Development* 63(8): 515–18.

Details an elaborate weighted point system to aid in determining authorship in research publications. Notes that weights for categories should be a group process and is less important than objective review of the contributions of those included.

Wolper. R. S. 1982. Why I edit — and keep editing — a journal. *Scholarly Publishing* 13(2): 149–55.

A subjective report by a journal editor as to why he edits: helping his colleagues with publishing, forcing him to know current scholarship, helping him to write better, allowing him to give something back to the field, and allowing him to join and continue a tradition.

Woodring, P. 1981. Writing about education. *Phi Delta Kappan* 62(7): 500–01.

Academic publishing lacks vigor, interest, and style. Author suggests: strong opening; visualizing audience; brevity — strong verbs, correct nouns; avoiding vogue words, euphemisms, and jargon; choosing the best topic — thoroughly familiar with but new; and rewriting.

———. 1982. Some thoughts on book reviewing. *Phi Delta Kappan* 63(6): 422.

In essence a book reviewer needs to answer the following questions: Are the author's ideas sound? Are they original? Are they significant or trivial? Do the conclusions logically follow from the evidence presented? Who should read this book? Reviewers should decline analysis of a book if their personal and educational background are not extensive enough to adequately judge the work.

Zirkel, P. A. 1978. Writing for education publications. *Journal of Teacher Education* 29(4): 69.

Thirteen steps for preparing and submitting manuscripts based on a seminar panel discussion of experts.

Zuckerman, H. 1967. Nobel laureates in science: Patterns of productivity, collaboration, and authorship. *American Sociological Review* 32(3): 391–403.

A total of forty-one Nobel laureates were studied. Found they start to publish earlier and continue longer than a matched sample. Median of 3.9 articles per year compared to 1.4 for matched group. The study examined collaboration and consequences of the prize.

Index